"As behavior analysts, how do you make your research, reports, and presentations most impactful? Learn to write well. Unfortunately, communicating effectively in writing is not something that comes easily for many of us, and there is tremendous variability in how these skills are addressed in graduate school, training, and supervision. That is why this manual is an essential read for behavior analysts wanting to hone their written communication. Whether you are a student, a practitioner, or a faculty member, you will find strategies and important considerations when writing for different audiences. This book is not just a manual; it is a mentor that many of us never had."

David Celiberti, PhD, BCBA-D, *Association for Science in Autism Treatment*

"*Writing Skills for Behavior Analysts* is everything a manual should be. It covers all the important topics, from communicating with humanity to navigating artificial intelligence. It offers understandable guidance for all domains of behavior analysis, from clinical to research to leadership. Above all, it is clear and useful. Thank you for this gem!"

Shahla Alai-Rosales, PhD, BCBA-D, CPBA-A, *Professor of Behavior Analysis, University of North Texas*

"Dr. Reinecke and colleagues have provided a needed resource in their comprehensive and systematic approach to writing for behavior analysts. It is essential to communicate effectively and compassionately while demonstrating professionalism when communicating with consumers, stakeholders, colleagues, and other professionals. This manual fills an important role as the only known comprehensive writing manual for behavior analysts that is suitable for students, practitioners, leaders, supervisors, researchers, and academics. The inclusion of practical checklists, examples and non-examples, self-reflection stations, and engaging practice questions ensures an active learning experience. This book is an indispensable tool and provides a robust framework for writing in every stage of a behavior analyst's career."

Vicki Madaus Knapp, PhD, BCBA-D, LBA (NY), *chairperson and associate professor, Department of Behavioral Science, Daemen University*

Writing Skills for Behavior Analysts

Writing Skills for Behavior Analysts provides a practical guidebook for students and clinicians. The book focuses on the importance of balancing technical information with compassionate delivery, providing guidance on writing that is meaningful across the scientific and human sides of the field.

Written by a group of clinicians, supervisors, and teaching faculty, the book targets eight key writing skills: writing as a human, writing as a student, writing as a clinician, writing as a leader, writing as a supervisor, writing as faculty, writing as a researcher and, finally, writing with artificial intelligence. By addressing each of these writing skills individually, the book is able to provide clear dos, don'ts, and examples in an easy-to-digest format.

This book will be an essential guide for any student of behavior analysis, as well as clinicians looking to hone their professional writing skills.

Dana Reinecke, PhD, BCBA-D, is a licensed psychologist, licensed behavior analyst, and faculty administrator.

Charissa Knihtila, PhD, BCBA-D, is a consultant and faculty member.

Jacob Papazian, PhD, BCBA-D, is a clinician and faculty member.

Celia Heyman, PhD, BCBA-D, is a clinician and faculty member.

Danielle Bratton, PhD, BCBA-D, is a licensed behavior analyst and faculty member.

Writing Skills for Behavior Analysts
A Practical Guide for Students and Clinicians

Edited by
Dana Reinecke, Charissa Knihtila,
Jacob Papazian, Celia Heyman and
Danielle Bratton

NEW YORK AND LONDON

Designed cover image: Getty Images © Scar1984

First published 2025
by Routledge
605 Third Avenue, New York, NY 10158

and by Routledge
4 Park Square, Milton Park, Abingdon, Oxon OX14 4RN

Routledge is an imprint of the Taylor & Francis Group, an informa business

© 2025 selection and editorial matter, Dana Reinecke, Charissa Knihtila, Jacob Papazian, Celia Heyman and Danielle Bratton; individual chapters, the contributors

The right of Dana Reinecke, Charissa Knihtila, Jacob Papazian, Celia Heyman and Danielle Bratton to be identified as the authors of the editorial material, and of the authors for their individual chapters, has been asserted in accordance with sections 77 and 78 of the Copyright, Designs and Patents Act 1988.

All rights reserved. No part of this book may be reprinted or reproduced or utilised in any form or by any electronic, mechanical, or other means, now known or hereafter invented, including photocopying and recording, or in any information storage or retrieval system, without permission in writing from the publishers.

Trademark notice: Product or corporate names may be trademarks or registered trademarks, and are used only for identification and explanation without intent to infringe.

Library of Congress Cataloging-in-Publication Data
Names: Reinecke, Dana, editor. | Knihtila, Charissa, editor. | Papazian, Jacob, editor. | Heyman, Celia, editor. | Bratton, Danielle, editor.
Title: Writing skills for behavior analysts : a practical guide for students and clinicians / edited by Dana Reinecke, Charissa Knihtila, Jacob Papazian, Celia Heyman, & Danielle Bratton.
Description: New York, NY : Roultedge, 2025. | Includes bibliographical references and index. |
Identifiers: LCCN 2024001161 (print) | LCCN 2024001162 (ebook) | ISBN 9781032732879 (hardback) | ISBN 9781032732848 (paperback) | ISBN 9781003463498 (ebook)
Subjects: LCSH: Behaviorism (Psychology) | Writing.
Classification: LCC BF199 .W758 2025 (print) | LCC BF199 (ebook) | DDC 150.19/43–dc23/eng/20240416
LC record available at https://lccn.loc.gov/2024001161
LC ebook record available at https://lccn.loc.gov/2024001162

ISBN: 978-1-032-73287-9 (hbk)
ISBN: 978-1-032-73284-8 (pbk)
ISBN: 978-1-003-46349-8 (ebk)

DOI: 10.4324/9781003463498

Typeset in Times New Roman
by Taylor & Francis Books

To my parents and to Bobby and David, for a lifetime of love and cheering me on. To my brothers, Anthony and David – always, all ways in my heart.

Dana Reinecke

This work is dedicated to Matt, Shayla, and Austin for their constant love, laughs, and support and to my colleagues who were on this ride from a crazy idea to an actual book.

Charissa Knihtila

This work is dedicated to the incredible colleagues who have supported this project whether they were cheering from the sidelines or getting their hands dirty with writing and editing.

Jacob Papazian

To my husband, Tony, and my children, Matthew and Brandon, for all the lessons you have taught me. To my past, present, and future students, I hope you will find this helpful.

Celia Heyman

To my incredible husband, Cody, and children, Jack, Julie, Isla, Alec, and Jane, for their constant encouragement. To my dedicated colleagues and your collective brilliance. With heartfelt gratitude for the support that fills both my personal and professional worlds.

Danielle Bratton

Contents

List of tables xiv
Acknowledgments xv
Introduction xvi
Contributors xxi

1 Writing (and Communicating) as a Human 1
　JACOB PAPAZIAN

　Social Media 1
　Public Perception 4
　Compassion and Empathy 6

2 Writing as a Student 11
　CHARISSA KNIHTILA, CHRISTINE SALAS, AND DANA REINECKE

　Email Communication 11
　Discussion Boards 13
　Assignments 16
　　Preparation for Assignments 16
　　Communication with Instructors About
　　　Assignments 17
　　Organizing Your Assignment 18
　　Critical Thinking 20
　　Grammar, Writing Style, and Honesty 22
　　Proofreading 24

Responding to Corrective Feedback on Assignments 25

3 Writing as a Clinician 30
CHARISSA KNIHTILA AND MICHELLE FUHR

Assessments 31
    Indirect Assessments 32
    Descriptive Assessments 33
    Functional Analysis (FA) 34
    Skills Assessment 36
Interpretations in Assessment Reports 38
    Analysis 38
    Recommendations 39
    Goals 40
Documentation of Services 41
    Progress Reports 42
    Session Notes 44
    Caregiver Session Notes 47

4 Writing as a Leader 51
DANIELLE BRATTON AND DANA REINECKE

Communicating with Caregivers 51
    Compassion-Focused Communication 51
    Performance Feedback and Recommendations 54
    Follow-Up Documentation 56
Communicating with Non-Behavioral Colleagues or Team Members 58
Communicating with Policy Makers 60
    Know the Problem 61
    Know Your Audience 62
    Make Comparisons 64
    Elevate the Right Voices 64
Communicating with Funders and Medical Providers 65
    Understanding Unique Needs 65
    Outcome Projections 66

    Customizing Proposals 66
    Evidence-Based Support 66
    Accessibility and Inclusivity 67
    Patient-Centered Approaches 67

5 Writing as a Supervisor   70
CELIA HEYMAN AND RENEE WOZNIAK

Structured Behavior Analytic Content 71
Supervision Documentation 72
    Supervision Contracts 73
    Meeting Documentation 74
Evaluations and Feedback 75
    Evaluating Supervisee Progress 76
    Evaluating the Effectiveness of Supervision 78

6 Writing as a Faculty Member   83
DANA REINECKE

Faculty-Produced Documents 83
    Syllabus 83
    Course Content 84
    Assignment Instructions 86
Providing Feedback 87

7 Writing as a Researcher   91
JULIANNE LASLEY, KAORI NEPO, AND DANA REINECKE

Literature Reviews 91
    Identify the Research Topic 92
    Identify Search Criteria 93
    Identify Articles for Review 94
    Organize the Articles 95
    Evaluate the Studies 96
    Synthesize Information: Putting it All
      Together 96

Research Proposals 98
  Justification for Research 99
  Research Plan 99
  Projected Outcomes 100
  Known Limitations and Delimitations 100
  Remember that the Research Process is Iterative 101
Grant Proposals 101
  Search for Grants 102
  Evaluate Resources 102
  Read and Understand 103
  Write Your Proposal 103
Disseminating Scholarly Work 105
  Conference Presentations 105
  Webinars 109
  Journal Articles 110

8 Writing as a Non-Human 115
DANIELLE BRATTON

How AI Can Help 115
  Automated Proofreading and Editing 115
  Natural Language Processing (NLP) 115
  Automated Report Generation 116
  Voice-to-Text Tools 116
Best Practices for Using AI in Writing 116
  Choose Your Tools Wisely 116
  Master the Tools 117
  Review AI-Generated Content 117
  Uphold Ethical Standards 117
  Combine Human Expertise with AI 117
  Stay Updated 117
Pitfalls and How Not to Use AI in Writing 118
  Don't Overrely on AI 118
  Ethical Concerns Matter 118
  Don't Skip the Review 118

    Understand How AI Works 118
    Security and Privacy Concerns 119
Conclusion 119

Appendix A: Words Matter	121
Appendix B: Recommended Responses for "How Would You Respond?"	123
Index	131

Tables

7.1 Sample table for organizing articles 96
A.1 Correct ways to use ABA terminology 121

Acknowledgments

This book was inspired by our own experiences as behavior analysts and writers at every level. We have been students, clinicians, supervisors, researchers, and faculty. In each of these roles, we have found mentors and models, and we thank those who taught and led us to this point. We hope that this manual provides some of the same inspiration to be not only strong writers, but also compassionate communicators as we practice our science.

We especially appreciate our clients and students for teaching us and shaping our behavior. We promise to continue to learn and grow and never forget what a privilege it is to be a part of your journeys.

Introduction

Behavior analysts work from a toolkit of knowledge and skills that can be used to alleviate suffering, improve quality of life, and enhance independence. We are uniquely skilled in identifying behavioral patterns and assessing factors contributing to behavior change. We are also trained to measure what makes people happy and what makes them unhappy, and we know how to help them achieve more of what makes them happy in safe, efficient, and productive ways. Behavior analysts can be some of the most fun people in the room because we can swiftly notice other people's behavior and adapt our own to encourage others to laugh, reach for more, and reciprocate interactions.

We are also specifically trained in how to teach others to implement behavioral strategies, because behavior analysts are rarely the only people involved in behavioral interventions. Suppose the intervention is designed to support a child. In that case, that child's family members, teachers, and other professionals or paraprofessionals are often more involved in implementing the intervention than the behavior analyst who designed it. If the intervention is for an adult, there may be staff responsible for carrying it out, or some adults will adopt the intervention themselves as self-management strategies.

Because behavior analysts are usually not the direct providers, we need to be highly competent communicators so that others can efficiently and effectively implement the strategies we design in our absence. This communication nearly always needs to occur at least partly in writing, and, under those circumstances, it must be clear, concise, and thorough. Behavior analysts must communicate in writing with both economy and detail, which is no small feat. Write too much, and your audience may need help to read or process it. Specifics may be missed. Write too little, and crucial details may not make it into the final product.

Another reason that behavior analysts need to be strong writers is that we usually need to present the results of assessments, the rationale for treatment, and treatment plans to funding sources and clients. The why of the intervention may be as important as the how because, with a strong justification, the intervention may be allowed to happen. Furthermore, ongoing progress reporting is essential for the continuation of funding and cooperation with treatment. As behavior analytic interventions are usually long-term strategies, there is a need to provide regular treatment updates to justify continuing services or terminating when no longer needed.

Most behavior analysts also spend a lot of their time preparing new professionals for the field, essentially working double-time at putting ourselves out of business by helping clients to not need interventions while training the next group of behavior analysts. Behavior analysts can afford to be so generous because we can help, on so many levels, so many different categories of people. It is to the benefit of the field and society at large for as many people as possible to practice behavior analysis with fluency and compassion to the highest ethical standards. Behavior analysts who are formal supervisors, mentors, and faculty members working with prospective behavioral professionals must also use and model effective written communication with trainees, supervisees, and students.

Finally, as effective as behavior analytic interventions are, there is still an acknowledged public relations problem in the field (Arthur et al., 2023; Freedman, 2016; Leaf et al., 2022). The current discussion around compassionate care (Denegri et al., 2023; Rodriguez et al., 2023; Taylor et al., 2019) and working collaboratively with other professionals (Kirby et al., 2022; Neuringer, 1991) stems in part from patterns of poor communication from some behavior analysts to those within and outside the field. Just as other professionals are more effective when they employ soft skills along with the tools of their trade, how behavior analysts are received depends on how they present themselves (Callahan et al., 2019).

Done correctly, with fidelity to the philosophy of behaviorism and resulting science, behavior analysis is a highly compassionate practice. Consider a definition of compassion that includes attending to the suffering of others, attempting to understand such suffering, and then implementing solutions geared towards alleviating suffering (Strauss et al., 2016). It is easy to identify those actions in the behavior analytic practices of observation, functional assessment, and interventions (Reinecke et al., 2023). Communication about behavior analytic assessment and recommendations must also be delivered compassionately, for complete fidelity with the Behavior Analysis Certification Board Code of Ethics (BACB, 2020) and what most agree is the highest aspiration for their practice.

Preparation and training for behavior analysts are largely focused on the philosophy, theories, and technologies of behavior change strategies. One area of focus that is lacking in the educational and training programs for behavior analysts is compassionate practices (LeBlanc et al., 2020). There has been recent emphasis on teaching soft skills and professionalism to aspiring behavior analysts, particularly in their interactions with clients, family members of clients, and other professionals (Callahan et al., 2019; Canon & Gould, 2022; Gatzunis et al., 2023; Reinecke et al., 2023; Rodriguez et al., 2023; Taylor et al., 2019). Writing skills may also not be highlighted in educational programs for behavior analysts, except for those relevant to scholarly activity. As important as writing is for the behavior analyst to deliver services effectively, efficiently, and compassionately, this is a large gap in training.

This handbook was created by a small group of behavior analysts representing a variety of behavior analysis professions. Most are faculty teaching aspiring behavior analysts in university settings, as well as supervisors and clinicians. With this manual, we attempt to model and teach effective behavior analytic writing by providing concise, clear, and helpful guidance across the many roles behavior analysts assume in their careers. This is not a resource for grammar, mechanics, or formatting; there are other guidebooks to support those skills. We also do not endorse specific templates or formats for behavior analytic products such as behavior intervention plans or functional assessment reports, as there are often specific requirements that vary by workplace or funding source. Instead, we seek to provide information about the type of information to include in your written products, guidance on how to write with compassion, examples and non-examples for your consideration, and opportunities for self-reflection where appropriate.

It is in our writing that behavior analysts demonstrate our technical proficiency in the science, together with our soft skills as compassionate practitioners. Our aim is to support behavior analytic writers in bringing together technical expertise and effective communication to reach their goals on individual, organizational, and social levels.

References

Arthur, S. M., Linnehan, A. M., Leaf, J. B., Russell, N., Weiss, M. J., Kelly, A. N., Saunders, M. S., & Ross, R. K. (2023). Concerns about ableism in applied behavior analysis: An evaluation and recommendations. *Education and Training in Autism and Developmental Disabilities, 58*(2), 127–143.

Behavior Analyst Certification Board. (2020). Ethics code for behavior analysts. https://bacb.com/wp-content/ethics-code-for-behavior-analysts/

Callahan, K., Foxx, R. M., Swierczynski, A., Aerts, X., Mehta, S., McComb, M. E., Nichols, S. M., Segal, G., Donald, A., & Sharma, R. (2019). Behavioral artistry: Examining the relationship between the interpersonal skills and effective practice repertoires of applied behavior analysis practitioners. *Journal of Autism and Developmental Disorders, 49*, 3557–3570. doi:10.1007/s10803-019-04082-1

Canon, L. F., & Gould, E. R. (2022). A preliminary analysis of the effects of clicker training and verbal instructions on the acquisition of relationship-building skills in two applied behavior analysis practitioners. *Behavior Analysis in Practice, 15*(2), 383–396. doi:10.1007/s40617-021-00555-x

Denegri, S., Cymbal, D., & Catrone, R. (2023). A multilevel framework for compassionate care in ABA: Approaches to cultivate a nurturing system. *Behavior Analysis in Practice.* doi:10.1007/s40617-023-00828-7

Freedman, D. H. (2016). Improving public perception of behavior analysis. *The Behavior Analyst, 39*(1), 89–95. doi:10.1007/s40614-015-0045-2

Gatzunis, K. S., Weiss, M. J., Ala'i-Rosales, S., Fahmie, T. A., & Syed, N. Y. (2023). Using behavioral skills training to teach functional assessment interviewing, cultural responsiveness, and empathic and compassionate care to students of applied behavior analysis. *Behavior Analysis in Practice.* doi:10.1007/s40617-023-00794-0

Kirby, M. S., Spencer, T. D., & Spiker, S. T. (2022). Humble behaviorism redux. *Behavior and Social Issues, 31*(1), 133–158. doi:10.1007/s42822-022-00092-4

LeBlanc, L. A., Taylor, B. A., & Marchese, N. V. (2020). The training experiences of behavior analysts: Compassionate care and therapeutic relationships with caregivers. *Behavior Analysis in Practice*, *13*(2), 387–393. doi:10.1007/s40617-019-00368-z

Leaf, J. B., Cihon, J. H., Leaf, R., McEachin, J., Liu, N., Russell, N., Unumb, L., Shapiro, S., & Khosrowshahi, D. (2022). Concerns about ABA-based intervention: An evaluation and recommendations. *Journal of Autism and Developmental Disorders*, *52*(6), 2838–2853. doi:10.1007/s10803-021-05137-y

Neuringer, A. (1991). Humble behaviorism. *The Behavior Analyst*, *14*(1), 1. doi:10.1007/bf03392543

Reinecke, D., Lasley, J., & Cirincione-Ulezi, N. (2023). Coursework in compassion and behavior analysis training programs. *Behavior Analysis in Practice*. doi:10.1007/s40617-023-00815-y

Rodriguez, K. A., Tarbox, J., & Tarbox, C. (2023). Compassion in autism services: A preliminary framework for applied behavior analysis. *Behavior Analysis in Practice*. doi:10.1007/s40617-023-00816-x

Strauss, C., Taylor, B. L., Gu, J., Kuyken, W., Baer, R., Jones, F., & Cavanagh, K. (2016). What is compassion and how can we measure it? A review of definitions and measures. *Clinical Psychology Review*, *47*, 15–27. doi:10.1016/j.cpr.2016.05.004

Taylor, B. A., LeBlanc, L. A., & Nosik, M. R. (2019). Compassionate care in behavior analytic treatment: Can outcomes be enhanced by attending to relationships with caregivers? *Behavior Analysis in Practice*, *12*(3), 654–666. doi:10.1007/s40617-018-00289-3

Contributors

Danielle Bratton, PhD, BCBA-D, is a Texas- and Louisiana-licensed behavior analyst and core faculty member at Capella University with over 19 years of experience in behavior analysis and a master's degree in professional counseling. Danielle has developed and taught online and hybrid graduate courses and created instructional programs for multiple universities. She owns Positive Behavior Change, LLC, providing ABA therapy, on-site and remote supervision, and consultation services in the areas of health and wellness, education, and organizational behavior management. Danielle has provided training and consultation to school districts, agencies, and families for individuals with disabilities. She collaborates with military organizations to provide resources and support to military families with children with disabilities. Danielle's current areas of research include instructional strategies for graduate learners, home education, and improving health-related behaviors. Danielle is a regional representative for the Louisiana Behavior Analysis Association (LABAA).

Michelle Fuhr, MS, BCBA, is a limited licensed psychologist and licensed behavior analyst in Michigan. She received her bachelor's and master's degrees from Western Michigan University, studying under Dr. Richard Malott. Michelle currently serves in roles of adjunct faculty for multiple universities, including Wayne State University, Capella University, and Macomb Community College. Michelle has a history of developing curriculum and teaching at the bachelor's and master's levels in behavior analysis programs for several university and college programs. She is the director of University Pediatricians Autism Center, in Clinton Township, Michigan, servicing clients of various ages and skill challenges. Michelle has been in the field of behavior analysis since 2005 and has presented at local and national conferences such as those held by the Behavior Analysis Association of Michigan (BAAM), Association of Behavior Analysis International (ABAI), and Women in Behavior Analysis (WIBA). She is currently seeking her PhD in behavior analysis through Capella University to pursue research and contribute to evidence-based practices.

Celia Heyman, PhD, BCBA-D, is a board-certified behavior analyst and a faculty member of Capella University's applied behavior analysis (ABA) graduate program. She received her doctorate in behavior analysis at Capella University. She has taught various ABA courses at Rider University and at Behavioral Momentum India. She has created and taught a supervision course at the Institute per la Ricerca in Italy. Celia obtained her training in public schools where she continues to provide consultation, focusing on the dissemination of practical functional assessment (PFA), skill-based treatment (SBT), and other assent-based interventions to address interfering behaviors. Her clinical skills include parent and staff training. She is a lead consultant and predoctoral fellow with FTF Behavioral Consulting. Her research interests include emerging learning instruction, acceptance and commitment training, and functional analysis. Celia is on the advisory board of the B. F. Skinner Foundation and is the Students Committee chairperson with the World Behavior Analysis Day Alliance. She was a guest editor of the *Behavior Analysis in Practice* 2023 special issue on compassion. In her spare time, Celia has cultivated an online study group for aspiring behavior analysts, reaching over 56,000 members worldwide.

Charissa Knihtila, PhD, BCBA-D, is a board-certified behavior analyst. She has taught online behavior analytic coursework at both the bachelors and masters level across several universities since 2013. Charissa is currently a Core Faculty member in the Department of Applied Behavior Analysis at Capella

List of contributors xxiii

University. Charissa has provided training and consultation to agencies related to training RBTs and direct staff and case supervision for individuals on the autism spectrum. Current areas of research include the application of behavior analytic strategies in the area of health and wellness and supporting students in an online teaching environment. Charissa has served on multiple committees with the California Association for Behavior Analysis (CalABA) including the professional standards committee and membership committee.

Julianne Lasley, EdD, BCBA-D, has dedicated over 20 years to the field of behavior analysis. Currently serving as the program director of the ABA program at Capella University, Julianne plays a crucial role in overseeing the curriculum and supporting student and faculty development. For the past decade, Julianne has been deeply involved in academia, functioning as a faculty leader in addition to mentoring doctoral students. Before transitioning to academia, Julianne applied the science of behavior analysis in various settings, including homes, schools, adult day care centers, and clinics. Her work in these settings involved providing support to children and adults with various disabilities. Furthermore, Julianne possesses experience and training in organizational behavior management, leveraging this knowledge to enhance performance and employee safety across different organizational settings. Her most recent research interests revolve around equity and inclusion in behavior analysis, college student persistence, feedback strategies for performance improvement, and leadership behaviors.

Kaori Nepo, PhD, BCBA-D, is a board-certified behavior analyst with doctoral designation and received her Master of Education in ABA from Temple University under Dr. Phil Hineline and her PhD in special education from Temple University under the guidance of Dr. Matthew Tincani. Dr. Nepo has worked in the field of behavior analysis for over 20 years as a consultant, researcher, and university faculty. Through her extensive clinical experience, she has supported numerous individuals with intellectual and developmental disability (IDD) as well as their families and educators. Dr. Nepo specializes in the use of commonly available technology in interventions for individuals with IDD and has multiple publications in this area. She has presented her research and clinical experience at local, national, and international conferences.

Jacob Papazian, PhD, BCBA-D, received an MS (2015) from Eastern Michigan University and a PhD (2022) from Capella University. He is a doctoral-level board certified behavior analyst (BCBA-D). In addition to a core faculty position at Capella University in the applied behavior analysis program, he also provides ongoing training to agencies in the areas of clinical quality assurance, culturally responsive leadership, and performance management. His current research focuses on social justice, diversity, equity, and inclusion, establishing effective technologies to teach leadership skills, and advancing pedagogical methods in higher education using behavior analysis and technology.

Dana Reinecke, PhD, BCBA-D, is a New York state licensed psychologist and licensed behavior analyst (LBA). She has developed and taught online, hybrid, and traditional face-to-face courses in bachelor's-, master's-, and doctoral-level programs across several universities in adjunct and full-time faculty roles since 1996. Dana is currently an assistant program director in the Department of Applied Behavior Analysis at Capella University, overseeing the PhD in behavior analysis program and mentoring doctoral learners. She is also co-owner of SupervisorABA, an online platform for BACB supervision, curriculum, and documentation. Dana has provided training and consultation to school districts, private schools, agencies, and families for individuals with disabilities. She has published her research in peer-reviewed journals, written chapters in published books, and co-edited books on ABA and autism. Current areas of research include use of technology to support students with and without disabilities and online teaching strategies for effective college and graduate education. Dana is a past president of the New York State Association for Behavior Analysis (NYSABA).

Christine Salas, MS, is from the Greater New York area. She holds a bachelor of science degree from Montclair State University and a master of science in psychology, specializing in applied behavior analysis, from Capella University. She is currently a PhD candidate

List of contributors xxv

in psychology with an area of study in behavior analysis at Capella University. While completing her doctorate, Christine obtained a higher education teaching certificate from Harvard University's Derek Bok Center for Teaching and Learning and a certificate in early education leadership (CEEL) through the Zaentz Professional Learning Academy at the Harvard Graduate School of Education. She also holds QBS safety-care certification in crisis prevention training and safety crisis management. Christine is a behavior analyst and clinical coordinator providing clients with intensive, one-on-one behavioral support and ABA therapy services in home-based, school, and community settings and social skills groups. Christine is a member of the National Society of Leadership and Success (NSLS) focus group. She is part of the Global Eagala Network as an Eagala-certified equine specialist and is Eagala's Research Committee's current vice chair and Bibliography Subcommittee lead. Christine has enjoyed volunteering for many years at local equine-assisted therapy facilities, assisting with occupational, adaptive, and speech-related programs for individuals with special needs. Christine's current area of research includes evaluating the effects of verbal behavior (VB) therapy for individuals diagnosed with autism during animal-assisted therapy (AAT), on and off horseback.

Renee Wozniak, PhD, BCBA-D is an Arizona LBA. She has worked in the field of special education and ABA in various capacities for over 25 years, in higher education, public schools, and home, clinical, and community settings. Across these settings she has developed, implemented, and supervised special education and ABA programs for individuals with autism and other disabilities and has trained and consulted with teachers, staff, college students, and families. She has taught both graduate and undergraduate courses in ABA, autism spectrum disorders, special education, and research for various universities and has served as a subject matter expert for master's and doctoral courses at Capella University. She has published and presented in the field and served two years on the board of directors for the Association for Science in Autism Treatment. Renee is currently a part-time faculty member in the Department of Applied Behavior Analysis at Capella University.

1 Writing (and Communicating) as a Human

Jacob Papazian

As a science, behavior analysis has seen an exponential increase in demand for services and the development of verified and accredited programs. As a direct result, it is to our benefit to determine the variables that will lead to a family choosing and maintaining behavior analytic interventions (Croen et al., 2017), maintain adequate line staff (Reid, 2017), and ensure the dissemination of the science with both accuracy and palatability (Kelly et al., 2019). Placement in the public sector requires a nuanced form of communication, one that is technical but approachable. Your language must demonstrate competence but refrain from alienating the audience or providing misinformation. With the increase of online social media platforms to reach consumers, these skills have become even more vital.

Social Media

Social media has quickly become the fastest way to communicate with a potential consumer, future employee, or professional colleague. Having an active media account provides you with a platform to disseminate information, network with colleagues, and establish relationships that may have never occurred otherwise. Consistent public posting of information regarding services, updates to best practices, and opportunities for employment and dissemination are now easier than ever and can elevate your personal and professional practice. Blog posts, for example, are a consistent way to drive online traffic to your practice and engage with the community on an international scale. However, without the process of peer review or supervision, you are responsible for what is done with that information.

DOI: 10.4324/9781003463498-1

Moreover, an often-underestimated aspect of sharing resources on social media is the critical importance of context. While the immediacy of these platforms encourages swift sharing, it's equally vital to offer contextual information about the content being shared. Providing a concise overview of the resource, outlining its purpose and intended audience, adds a layer of clarity for those engaging with the content. This contextualization aids in making the shared material more accessible and relevant, as it helps potential readers quickly grasp whether the content aligns with their interests or needs. Equally imperative is citing the source of the resource, facilitating a pathway for others interested in delving deeper into the subject matter. Such practice not only elevates the overall credibility of the shared content but also fosters an environment of transparency and mutual learning among participants.

Furthermore, as the volume of information circulating on social media platforms continues to surge, the need for effective moderation becomes increasingly evident. With the diversity of perspectives and opinions that these platforms accommodate, maintaining a semblance of professional decorum is essential. Establishing clear guidelines for moderation ensures that discussions remain constructive and respectful, enhancing the overall value of the shared resources and interactions. By actively curating conversations and intervening when necessary, professionals can foster an environment where the exchange of ideas remains fruitful and conducive to mutual growth. Effective moderation not only safeguards the quality of interactions but also serves to cultivate a sense of professionalism and accountability among participants.

Social media can allow for opportunities to share resources and provide professional development. However, striking a balance between disseminating resources and maintaining confidentiality/pursuing best practices can be a challenge. It is strongly recommended that another certificant serve as an editor and a non-certificant serve as a "beta reader" to determine if the material is analytically sound but also approachable and non-directive in orientation. Focus the analysis on the underlying core principles in language that are reasonable for your target audience. When appropriate, link additional resources for training and development once they are adequately vetted by you or another trusted certificant. Be certain to always include a properly formatted references section!

Lastly, in the realm of social media engagement, privacy stands as a critical concern. While professionals exchange insights and resources and engage in discussions, safeguarding sensitive information and respecting personal data boundaries are essential. Balancing transparency with privacy ensures that professionals contribute to the discourse while retaining control over shared content. Being cautious about oversharing, especially when discussing specific cases, is important. Checking and using appropriate privacy settings and controls and refraining from revealing personally identifiable details are essential steps to maintain personal and professional integrity.

Do:

- Have an online social presence.
- Actively engage in your online presence and post with some regularity.
- Network with other professionals.
- Maintain collegial and professional interactions over the keys.
- Provide scholarly references to support your posts when appropriate.
- Moderate your social media presence and ensure that information being discussed is accurate, compassionate, and beneficial to the discussion.

Don't:

- Post testimonials that were solicited by anyone in your practice.
- Share specifics related to clinical progress or personal information of any current or former clients.
- Provide feedback or potential clinical recommendations regarding specific situations or practices.
- Allow posts on your social media page(s) that are incongruent with best practices in behavior analysis.
- Respond defensively to individuals who post a negative review.

Public Perception

Terry Goodkind once said "reality is irrelevant. Perception is everything." The first step to adequately managing your public persona, particularly through written discourse, is remembering your audience and catering to their vernacular. Blog posts and other community interactions with non-behavior-analytic practitioners or caregivers that are written like a behavior analytic thesis are less likely to be received well. Using culturally responsive language not only gives your writing tremendous ethos but also enhances the overall perception of your competence (Dunn & Andrews, 2015). Practice self-awareness by transcribing internal private events without editing them to help identify any potential patterns of bias (Gün, 2011; Yip, 2006). Be mindful of these patterns as you engage verbally in the behavior analytic community.

Effective communication within any field, including behavior analysis, hinges on the ability to convey complex ideas with clarity and conciseness. While precision is vital in behavior analytic discourse, it's equally important to avoid unnecessary jargon or convoluted explanations when engaging with non-practitioners or caregivers. Just as behavior analysts strive for clarity in their interventions, the same principle applies to written communication. By employing straightforward language and providing relatable examples, you bridge the gap between technical expertise and accessible understanding. Remember that the goal is not to compromise accuracy but to convey information in a manner that invites curiosity and fosters a mutual exchange of knowledge.

Credibility is the cornerstone of any professional's reputation. In the realm of behavior analysis, this entails demonstrating a deep understanding of the field's principles and practices. To establish credibility, consistently showcase your expertise through well-researched content, thoughtful insights, and a track record of contributions to the field. This could involve publishing articles in reputable journals, speaking at conferences, and collaborating on research projects. As you become more visible, it's essential to maintain your credibility by staying up-to-date with the latest research, responding to feedback, and admitting when you don't have all the answers. Transparency about the evolving nature of the field and your commitment to continuous learning fosters trust and enhances your reputation.

Respectful communication lies at the heart of building strong relationships within the behavior analytic community and beyond. Acknowledge and value diverse perspectives, experiences, and contributions. This not only demonstrates inclusivity but also enriches the quality of discourse. Avoid dismissive or condescending language, even when discussing differing viewpoints. When engaging with others, prioritize active listening and empathy. Recognize that everyone brings unique insights, and constructive conversations thrive when participants feel their dignity is upheld. In written discourse, refrain from personal attacks or assumptions, and instead focus on the ideas being presented. By fostering an environment of respect, you contribute to a culture of collaboration and shared growth within the field.

In essence, effective communication within the behavior analytic community necessitates understanding your audience, conveying ideas with clarity, maintaining credibility, and promoting respect. These principles, combined with an active presence in both professional and broader spheres, enable behavior analysts to contribute meaningfully, drive positive change, and elevate the field's perception. Just as perception shapes reality, thoughtful and considerate communication shapes the perception of your role and impact within the behavior analytic community.

It would be remiss to discuss public perception without discussing your need to be involved in the professional sector as well as the greater field of dissemination. Being part of the conversation in your local professional arena provides you with the ability to be involved in grassroots phases of change for our field. Ensure that you are visible at strategic moments throughout your time in the professional spotlight, as it were. Focus your efforts on advancing the field by joining your state's ABAI chapter or other professional organization. If you are interested in a specific sub-discipline, join a relevant special interest group (SIG) and become more involved in its efforts to enhance the field. Actively participate in regional and national conferences through attendance and submission of original research. Remember that a poster presentation can capture the imagination and academic creativity of another individual just as easily as a seminar or workshop. Always ask for feedback and actively implement it as you continue to present. Just ensure that you are not overextending your schedule or overcommitting yourself to a point where you are unable to adequately meet expectations.

Do:

- Use language that is appropriate within the context of the public discourse.
- Actively participate in regional conferences through attendance and research.
- Join your local ABAI chapter or other professional behavioral organization.
- Support local agencies through advocacy and providing professional development as you are able.
- Set aside time each week to devote to your public persona accounts.
- Respond to those who reach out.

Don't:

- Make commitments that are not within your ability or feasible with your schedule (i.e., don't say yes to everything).
- Oversell yourself or offer services that are not within the scope of your practice or area of expertise.
- Overuse behavioral jargon.

Compassion and Empathy

The concepts of empathy and compassion are components of a robust literature base in the contextual behavioral sciences (e.g., Goetz & Simon-Thomas, 2017). Non-behavior analytic research has indicated that medical doctors who engage in "compassionate care" have improved outcomes with patients, but this has yet to be further researched by behavior analysts (Taylor et al., 2019). Compassion can be defined as the synergy of empathetic behavior (e.g., perspective taking of an emotional response) with an observable behavioral response (e.g., normalizing an emotional response by saying, "I would have been mad too"). Although it sounds mentalistic, compassion can be described as a response class that we routinely engage in.

For example, a behavior analyst interfacing with a patient who is crying after describing the recent death of a beloved family pet must be able to respond to cues to discriminate the potential internal events (e.g., emotional experiences). Through a series of coordinated relations based on the behavior analyst's own experience with loss, covert behavior could be established, such as, "If I were you, I would be very sad right now," owing to the similarity in stimulus events. Using evidence-based techniques, such as motivational interviewing, provides a framework for you to engage in meaningful verbal interactions with people regarding behavior change while maintaining empathetic responses that enhance therapeutic alliance to evoke change (Magill et al., 2010).

Identifying this framework within the context of your writing is vital to effective verbal and vocal communication. Asking for an individual's preferences regarding their pronouns or identity- versus disability-first language enhances therapeutic alliance (Ardito & Rabellino, 2011). Including the individual in this decision-making process not only enhances rapport but is also part of the conversation regarding reducing stigma, as scholarly writing has historically only used person-first language for individuals diagnosed with a severe disability but not commonly for individuals without some type of chronic diagnosis (Gernsbacher, 2017). The inclusion of autoclitics within your writing (e.g., if you have the time, please, it would be great, etc.) also enhances delivery by softening responses and providing a more collaborative approach rather than a directional or authoritarian one. Providing adequate and reasonable expectations of those you supervise further enhances your writing by establishing your written word as a discriminative stimulus. If expectations or formal communication consistently result in a state of extinction (i.e., no reinforcement), future correspondence may serve as a stimulus-delta, resulting in avoidance behavior.

Do:

- Use motivational interviewing and other evidence-based compassion-oriented techniques.
- Assess preference regarding person-first language and follow the audience preference.

- Introduce yourself with your pronouns and ask what pronouns the other person uses.
- Be flexible with others.
- Say please and thank you.
- Express gratitude and appreciation.
- Answer questions politely.

Don't:

- Be a doormat: There is a difference between being compassionate and being a pushover.
- Demand perfection from others.
- Demand perfection from yourself.
- Provide unrealistic expectations.
- Respond defensively to feedback regarding your performance.

Self-Reflection Station

1 Reflect on your current social media presence as a behavior analyst. Are you actively using social media to disseminate information and engage with your audience? If not, how could you start leveraging these platforms to share updates on best practices and job opportunities?
2 Consider your involvement in the professional sector and behavior analytic community. Are you actively participating in conferences and workshops, or joining special interest groups to advance the field? Reflect on how you can strategically be more visible and contribute to grassroots efforts for positive change.

Practice: How Would You Respond?

Compare your responses to our recommendations at the end of this book.

1 After a parent receives an autism diagnosis for their child, you and a supervisee are having your first interview with the family. After the parents express their concerns regarding their child's development, your supervisee says, "Don't worry; your

child will catch up eventually," and continues by asking questions about their schedule. How would you write out your feedback to your supervisee in your notes for them to review and reference in the future regarding compassionate care?

2 Sarah is a behavior analyst known for her expertise but she struggles with an abrasive online presence. Sarah frequently engages in debates on social media, often dismissing alternative viewpoints. Her interactions lack collegiality, which has led to strained relationships with fellow professionals. As a result, her valuable insights on behavior analysis often get overshadowed by the confrontational tone. You come across a recent exchange on social media where Sarah engages in a heated debate about the use of extinction in clinical care. In an attempt to model a more compassionate response, write a brief response to Sarah's comment.

References

Ardito, R. B., & Rabellino, D. (2011). Therapeutic alliance and outcome of psychotherapy: Historical excursus, measurements, and prospects for research. *Frontiers in Psychology, 2*, 270. doi:10.3389/fpsyg.2011.00270

Croen, L. A., Shankute, N., Davignon, M., Massolo, M. L., & Yoshida, C. (2017). Demographic and clinical characteristics associated with engagement in behavioral health treatment among children with autism spectrum disorders. *Journal of Autism and Developmental Disorders, 47*, 3347–3357. doi:10.1007/s10803-017-3247-5

Dunn, D. S., & Andrews, E. E. (2015). Person-first and identity-first language: Developing psychologists' cultural competence using disability language. *American Psychologist, 70*(3), 255. doi:10.1037/a0038636

Gernsbacher, M. A. (2017). Editorial perspective: The use of person-first language in scholarly writing may accentuate stigma. *Journal of Child Psychology and Psychiatry, 58*(7), 859–861. doi:10.31234/osf.io/7wxea

Goetz, J. L., & Simon-Thomas, E. (2017). The landscape of compassion: Definitions and scientific approaches. *The Oxford Handbook of Compassion Science, 1*, 3–15.

Gün, B. (2011). Quality self-reflection through reflection training. *ELT journal, 65*(2), 126–135. doi:10.1093/elt/ccq040

Kelly, M. P., Martin, N., Dillenburger, K., Kelly, A. N., & Miller, M. M. (2019). Spreading the news: History, successes, challenges and the ethics of effective dissemination. *Behavior Analysis in Practice, 12*, 440–451. doi:10.1007/s40617-018-0238-8

Magill, M., Apodaca, T. R., Barnett, N. P., & Monti, P. M. (2010). The route to change: Within-session predictors of change plan completion in a motivational interview. *Journal of Substance Abuse Treatment*, *38*(3), 299–305. doi:10.1016/j.jsat.2009.12.001

Reid, D. H. (2017). Competency-based staff training. In *Applied behavior analysis advanced guidebook* (pp. 21–40). Academic Press.

Taylor, B. A., LeBlanc, L. A., & Nosik, M. R. (2019). Compassionate care in behavior analytic treatment: Can outcomes be enhanced by attending to relationships with caregivers? *Behavior Analysis in Practice*, *12*(3), 654–666. doi:10.1007/s40617-018-00289-3

Yip, K. S. (2006). Self-reflection in reflective practice: A note of caution. *British Journal of Social Work*, *36*(5), 777–788. doi:10.1093/bjsw/bch323

2 Writing as a Student

Charissa Knihtila, Christine Salas, and Dana Reinecke

Behavior analysis students must produce many different types of written documents, from email communication with faculty to lengthy research papers (Ondrusek, 2012). Behavior analysis studies may begin in undergraduate education and extend through doctoral programs. At any level of study, behavior analysis students may find themselves unfamiliar with the technical and sometimes confusing writing required for their assignments. The language associated with applied behavior analysis (ABA) may be unfamiliar, and students may grapple with new vocabulary and different usages for familiar terms. Additionally, behavior analytic writing must be clear and concise (Luiselli, 2023), which can be challenging for students taught to write expansively and use a thesaurus in other coursework. This chapter provides guidance on written communication with instructors and fellow students.

Email Communication

One of the main forms of communication with a professor, academic advisor, peer, or any other individual related to your degree program is email (Aguilar-Roca et al., 2009; Rahman et al., 2008). This is a simple way for you to ask questions or get information regarding your academic progress. Email will also document your conversations with a permanent product (Aguilar-Roca et al., 2009). When you are communicating via email, there are a few important things to consider:

- Use proper grammar. Emails are not text messages, even if they are sent from a mobile device. Proper punctuation and grammar will help to set a professional tone.
- Indicate the specific topic in the subject line.
- Be clear and concise in your message by stating your problem or question quickly and completely.
- Start your email with a professional greeting.
- End your email with your name.
- Do not expect an immediate response. It is customary to allow for a minimum of 24 hours for the person you emailed to respond during the work week, and longer if you email on a Friday or over a weekend.

Example:

> Subject Line: Advising request regarding schedule
> Hi Evie,
> I wanted to set up an advisement meeting next week to ask some questions about my schedule for next semester. The best days and times for me are Monday and Wednesday between 1pm and 3pm Central time. I think 30 minutes should be plenty of time. Do either of those days work for you?
> Thanks,
> Lola Student

Non-example:

> Subject Line: Meeting
> I need to talk to you can we meet

Do:

- Use the subject line to appropriately convey content.
- Respectfully address your email to the correct name of the person you are contacting.
- Use a polite and respectful tone.
- Include your name at the end.
- Check spelling, grammar, and punctuation.

Don't:

- Use text lingo, slang, shorthand, or incomplete sentences.
- Allow your emotions to overcome and impact your writing or become argumentative.
- Expect immediate responses (typically allow for 24–48 hours).
- Send multiple sequential emails on the same or different topics.

Discussion Boards

As a student, you may engage in online discussion forums for your coursework. These discussions are typically meant for you to engage with the course content or share opinions on a selected topic (Galikyan & Admiraal, 2019). Discussions work best when engagement occurs over a few interactions, so remember to respond to your peers' posts and to be communicative in return when they respond to your posts. It may be tempting to simply write "I agree" or "Good point" on a peer's post, but this does not lead to more dialogue. Taking the time to thoughtfully respond to a peer or to answer when your instructor responds to your post can lead to an engaging, meaningful interaction, despite the asynchronous nature of discussion boards. Your response may include affirmation, more information, and thoughtful questions to encourage continued discussion.

Remember that, although this can be a casual space, your tone should remain courteous in your original post and any response posts to your peers and instructor. If you are in a situation where you disagree with a fellow classmate's post, remember to engage in a constructive manner, as opposed to a critical and judgmental one (Chen et al., 2021). Not all students have the same background, and discussion forums are usually meant not only for the instructor to evaluate your knowledge, but also to allow for learning from peers.

As online educational technologies have evolved, some discussion board environments may feel more like social media platforms. Instructors/professors may use these discussions not only to build comfort with content, but also to increase the feeling of community across students in the course. In this situation, it is easy to fall into the traps often associated with social media such as presenting yourself very informally or engaging in unprofessional interactions with others. Remember that, although these discussion environments are more casual and may include prompts that allow for sharing more about your personal journey (e.g., wins for the week, funny memes), this is still an academic setting. If you feel comfortable, you can share aspects of your personal life that fit within the discussion prompt. While courseroom discussions are private among the students enrolled in that course, be sure to consider the aspects discussed earlier in this book related to both public perception and social media writing.

Discussion response example:

> Hi Tori, What a great point about how extinction may be the most effective intervention, but not necessarily the best choice. I agree with you that for SIB with an escape function, extinction may be highly effective, but would not be appropriate to implement due to the potential risk of harm to the client. I think that the same could be true for physical aggression toward others, regardless of the age of the child. You mention that you had a 2-year-old client who engaged in physical aggression. Do you think extinction might also pose a risk for them or others in their environment? I've encountered situations in which physical aggression from a young child toward an adult was unlikely to cause harm, but there was higher risk to peers and the client alike if the peer was to respond with physical aggression! Thanks for giving me something challenging to think about!
> – Jack Student

Discussion response non-example:

> Hi Tori, Nice post! I agree that extinction is beneficial and can be unethical. I think you were wrong about extinction for aggression, though. I look forward to reading more of your posts.

Disagreeing with a peer example:

> Hi Lyra,
> I appreciate your thoughtful post on the use of extinction in clinical care. I agree with some of your points, but I

Writing as a Student 15

respectfully disagree with others. First, I agree with you that extinction can be a very effective treatment for some disorders, such as phobias and obsessive-compulsive disorder (OCD). For example, a person with a fear of spiders may be exposed to spiders in a safe and controlled environment, starting with pictures of spiders and gradually moving up to live spiders. Over time, the person's fear should decrease as they learn that the spiders do not pose a real threat. However, I disagree with your suggestion that extinction should be used for all disorders. For example, extinction has been shown to be less effective for disorders such as anxiety and depression. Additionally, extinction can be a very difficult and distressing process for some clients. It is important to carefully consider the client's individual needs and preferences before deciding whether or not to use extinction.

Finally, I would like to add that extinction is not without its risks. For example, some studies have shown that extinction can lead to increased aggression in some clients. Additionally, extinction can be upsetting for clients with a history of trauma. It is important for clinicians to be aware of these risks and to monitor their clients closely during extinction therapy. Overall, I believe that extinction is a valuable tool that can be used to help some clients overcome their fears and compulsions. However, it is important to use extinction carefully and ethically.

– Rowan Hawthorne

Disagreeing with a peer non-example:

Dear Aaliyah,

I read your post on the use of extinction in clinical care, and I have to say, I'm disappointed. It's clear that you don't understand extinction therapy, and your post is full of misconceptions. You claim that extinction is "cruel" and "inhumane." That's simply not true. Extinction is a safe and effective treatment that has been used for decades to help people overcome their fears and phobias. In fact, extinction is often less distressing than other forms of therapy, such as cognitive-behavioral therapy (CBT).

You also claim that extinction is "ineffective." That's also not true. There is a wealth of research that supports the effectiveness of extinction therapy. For example, a recent study found that extinction was more effective than CBT for treating spider phobia. Overall, your post is a complete and utter misrepresentation of the facts. I urge you to do your research before posting such uninformed and misleading information.

– Kai River Smith

Do:

- Engage in cordial discussion with an open mind about controversial topics.
- Provide explanation for your agreement or disagreement with a peer's post.
- Remain professional in your correspondence, even if a more casual setting has been built in the courseroom.

Don't:

- Overshare by providing details about your personal life not related to the discussion.
- State blatantly that another student is wrong.

Assignments

Preparation for Assignments

Students are often asked to complete written assignments that require you to research, summarize, synthesize, and support your own statements in full written paragraphs. To be efficient in assignment writing, it is best to prepare before you start actually writing. Here are seven steps to help you prepare for writing your assignment:

- Think about the purpose of the assignment. What understanding or skill are you being asked to demonstrate in this assignment? Check to see if specific competencies are aligned with the assignment.

- Read all instructions that are listed in the course. Note areas where you have questions.
- Review the scoring guide or rubric. Note if your questions about the instructions are answered in the scoring guide.
- If a template is provided, use it.
- Using the information from the instructions and rubric, set up an outline of your assignment. This should include the headings you plan to use and potential bullet points of the material that needs to be covered under each heading.
- Before you start writing, check each point of the scoring guide or rubric to ensure that it is covered in your outline.
- Review the APA manual and follow correct APA formatting.

Communication with Instructors About Assignments

As you are completing your work for classes, you may have questions regarding the specific expectations for assignments, exams, or projects. Before contacting your instructor with a question, be sure that you have:

- Read the instructions or expectations provided in the syllabus or online courseroom.
- Reviewed the scoring guide or rubric and any samples provided.
- Reviewed all supplemental material provided to you (e.g., previous emails between you and the instructor, links to outside materials in the courseroom).

If you have completed these steps and your question is not answered, you may engage in written communication with your instructor to ensure that you are completing the work correctly. Use concise and professional language and include an appropriate subject line that identifies the purpose of your email. Consider all of your questions before sending one email. It can be helpful to draft your email and wait before sending it. This gives you time to gather and organize your thoughts and to re-evaluate the emotional tone of your message. Once the draft is complete, proofread it carefully, make any necessary changes, and formulate one clear and concise email.

Example:

Subject Line: Week 4 Assignment 1
Hi Professor Adams,
I am working on the assignment due this week and have a question. I saw on the instructions that we need to provide three behavioral definitions. Should the behaviors that I am defining all be exhibited by the same person or can they be behaviors that I observed from different people?
Thank you,
Manny Student

Non-example:

Subject Line: HELP ME!
Hey,
I am so confused about this assignment! It says that we need to define behaviors, but I don't know which ones! I need you to tell me which behaviors I'm supposed to define.

Organizing Your Assignment

The order of information in your assignment is just as important as the content. Organization is as critical within paragraphs as on a higher level across the assignment as a whole. Use an outline to ensure that you are answering the assignment instructions in a coherent, easy-to-follow manner. Writing can be structured in several different ways, but what is most important is that it is organized intentionally. You may organize around specific themes, or from general to specific information. You may also organize by when events occurred in time.

Breaking your writing into paragraphs helps to convey the organization of your assignment. Each paragraph should have a purpose and should follow the previous paragraph in a meaningful way. Similarly, each sentence should introduce new information and follow the prior sentence logically.

Example:

Differential reinforcement of incompatible behaviors (DRI) is a schedule of reinforcement that can be used to increase the frequency of desired behavior by reinforcing behavior that is incompatible with the undesired behavior. DRI is a safe and effective intervention that is often used to address a variety of unwanted behaviors, such as aggression, self-injurious behavior, and disruptive behavior. One example of how DRI can be used is to help a child who is screaming for attention. The parent could give the child attention whenever the child is sitting quietly, and ignore when the child is screaming. Over time, the child will learn that sitting quietly is the best way to get attention.

DRI can be challenging to implement, but it is a valuable tool that can be used to help children and adults overcome a variety of unwanted behaviors. It is important to note that DRI is not a one-size-fits-all approach, and what works for one child may not work for another. Additionally, DRI can be time-consuming and requires consistent reinforcement from the caregiver.

Non-example:

DRI procedures are a type of reinforcement that can be used to increase the frequency of a desired behavior by reinforcing a behavior that is incompatible with the undesired behavior. However, it is important to note that DRI is not a one-size-fits-all approach, and what works for one child may not work for another. Additionally, DRI can be time-consuming and requires consistent reinforcement from the caregiver. DRI is safe and effective, but it can be challenging to implement. For example, if a child is screaming to get attention, a parent could use DRI to reinforce the child for sitting quietly. The parent would give the child attention whenever the child is sitting quietly, and ignore when the child is screaming. Over time, the child will learn that sitting quietly is the best way to get attention. DRI can be used to address a variety of unwanted behaviors, such as aggression, self-injurious behavior, and disruptive behavior. It is a valuable tool that can be used to help children and adults overcome a variety of unwanted behaviors.

Critical Thinking

The level of analysis you are asked to perform will vary by the assignment. As you are preparing for your assignments, look for the verbs in the instructions to determine what is expected. If the assignment instructions ask you to define, describe, or summarize, your task is to explain information as it is presented from other sources. If the assignment instructions ask you to compare or contrast, synthesize, or analyze, your task is to manipulate information from other sources to draw a conclusion. Following are some descriptions of the type of work you may produce for assignments using these different words:

- **Define or describe:** Verbs such as define or describe indicate that you should explain a concept, behavior, term, or other variable in your own words. Definitions and descriptions should be written succinctly and concisely, with as much precision as possible. If you are defining a term or concept, cite a source for your definition. If you are defining behavior, it is only necessary to cite a source if the definition is not your own. For example, if defining the term "negative reinforcement," you should cite a source because you did not invent the term or what it means. If the assignment is to define a behavior of your choice, such as dancing, you don't need to cite a source because you will invent the definition. If, however, you use a definition for dancing that was established in a book or article, you should then cite that source.
- **Summarize:** When summarizing research, you are describing one study at a time. Summarizing is often used in creating an annotated bibliography or gathering research to support an intervention. The details of the design, participants, and results are all written in your own words with a proper citation. Summarizing is important in assignment writing because it provides detail pertaining to specific articles and shows your instructor that you are able to identify key factors and write in detail about specific studies. The level of detail you provide in your summary will depend on the assignment instructions and what is most important about the study that you are summarizing. It is usually not necessary or appropriate to list very

specific details in a summary, such as the ages or IQs of participants, or the specific data included in the results. Instead, you should make summative statements that provide enough information for the reader to understand the study, without getting bogged down in details.
- **Compare and contrast:** Sometimes, your assignment will involve analyzing information from more than one source. A common way of doing this is to compare and contrast those sources of information. Comparing is done by pointing out what is similar or common between the sources, and contrasting is done by explaining what is different between the sources. Your choice of variables to compare and contrast is important for supporting the overall meaning of your writing. You should look for the information in the articles that are most relevant to the assignment and explain how they are similar and different in those areas. Thoughtful organization is also important when comparing and contrasting. Your work here is to convey a message about the sources, so be sure that you frame that message in a coherent manner.
- **Synthesize:** When synthesizing research, you are reading multiple sources on one subject, finding common factors across all sources, and developing a new thought from all this information. Think of synthesizing as taking a group of ingredients and combining them to create a dish that did not exist before. Flour, butter, eggs, and sugar can be synthesized to create cake. In writing, that means that you take information from different sources and present that information in such a way that your reader can agree with you on your unique conclusion about this information. Synthesis is a step beyond summarizing or gathering information, requiring you to draw a conclusion or identify a next question or step in research. Synthesis is important in assignment writing because it reduces the repetition of common factors found within the research and shows your instructor that you are able to read the research, find the different factors that match each other, and write about those factors in a way that incorporates the information from multiple sources.
- **Analyze:** Behavior analysts are skilled in analyzing data, but written material can also be analyzed. Assignments may require

you to analyze articles to demonstrate your competence in understanding content. You might analyze a research article by briefly summarizing key points from the article and then identifying strengths and limitations in the research design, procedures, and analysis of data. It is also possible to analyze groups of studies or areas of research by assessing what questions have and have not been answered across different articles.

Grammar, Writing Style, and Honesty

Correct grammar, punctuation, and sentence structure are important in all areas of writing. Behavior analysts write in clear, concise, and objective language whenever possible (Kazemi et al., 2018). Avoid using unnecessary extra words, or special "fancy" words. When you use behavior analytic terminology, be sure that you are using it correctly. See a list of common errors in behavior analytic terms at the end of this book.

Scholarly writing should be direct and use an active, rather than passive, voice. If you are describing research that has already been conducted, from articles that you have read, use the past tense. If you are proposing future study or analysis, use the future tense.

You should usually avoid first-person perspectives in assignments, unless the instructions specifically note that an opinion should be offered. Instead, you will mostly be expected to write about factual information with proper citation of sources. Using citations increases the scholarly tone of your writing and avoids plagiarism by giving credit to the original source.

Be very careful not to engage in plagiarism, which is when ideas or words are used without giving credit to the original source. Plagiarism does not have to be deliberate; even if it occurs unintentionally, plagiarism is a serious offense and can have repercussions for your academic and professional career. Because most of the writing you will do as a student will be based upon the work of others, you will do a lot of paraphrasing. Here are some steps and suggestions for paraphrasing:

- Read the original text carefully and understand its meaning. Do not attempt to paraphrase until you are sure you understand what you are reading.

- Identify the main ideas of the text. Pretend you are explaining this reading to someone who has not read it and who has no training in this area. How would you tell them about it at a very high and simple level? It is strongly recommended that you do not copy and paste from the reading into your assignment with the intention of changing the words later. Instead, make notes as bullet points.
- Edit the bullet points into sentences and paragraphs using your own words to restate the main ideas. When paraphrasing, it is important to use your own words and sentence structure. Do not simply substitute synonyms for the words in the original text.
- Use different words and phrases from those used in the original text. This does not mean that you have to use obscure or technical language. Instead, use words that you commonly use in your own vocabulary.
- Cite the source that you are paraphrasing from. Use the most current APA formatting or any other style required by your academic program. Citations usually include the last name of the first author and the year of publication, and may be part of the sentence or added in parentheses at the end of the sentence.

Always aim to paraphrase information from the sources you are citing rather than using direct quotes. The only reason to use a direct quote is if there is something particularly meaningful about the way the information is stated. Restating things in your own words demonstrates competence with the material. Ensure the salience of your quote by following proper APA formatting: Put quotation marks around the words that you have copied and state the name of the author, year of publication, and page number where the quote was copied from.

Example:

> Students can increase scores on assignments by reading the scoring guide thoroughly and using that scoring guide to self-grade. It is suggested that students who self-grade are more cautious about including all requirements from the scoring guide and that they grade their work more harshly than the instructor.
> (Author, 2023)

Non-example:

> I think that best practice related to doing well on assignments is to read the scoring guide and use it to grade your own paper. I also believe that the student is likely to grade themselves harder than the instructor will, which makes the students work harder to include everything from the scoring guide.

Proofreading

No matter how confident you are in your writing and in automated grammar and spell checkers, proofread your assignments! Never submit an assignment until after you have read it over more than once. Here are some suggested steps for proofreading your work:

- Read through your work once for content and organization. Did you include all the information that you wanted to include, and does the order of information make sense? Does every paragraph have a purpose, and does every sentence add something new? Remove any redundant sentences and reorganize your paragraphs for the most logical flow.
- Score your own work using the rubric or scoring guide. Be very honest in your assessment. Did you earn the grade you wanted on this assignment? Make any corrections needed to demonstrate your competence through this assignment.
- Read through your work again and ensure that all citations are included and that you did indeed paraphrase rather than copying. If your academic program provides a plagiarism checker, use it. Ensure that all citations have a corresponding full reference on the reference page, and that all references on the reference page are cited in the assignment. If you copied references from other sources, proofread them to ensure that they meet APA formatting standards.
- Use technology to check your grammar and spelling, including checkers that are integrated into your word processing software and other external services. Don't just trust the computer suggestions, however. Review each suggested error carefully to determine how best to address the suggestion.

- Read through your assignment once more, out loud, and listen to each sentence to ensure that it makes sense and there are no extra or missing words.

Do:

- Read all assignment instructions first.
- Review the scoring guide/rubric closely.
- Self-grade using the score guide/rubric.
- Check spelling, grammar, punctuation, and APA formatting.
- Use citations to support your statements.
- Pay attention to the verbs used in the assignments.

Don't:

- Plagiarize or take credit for others' work.
- Misuse behavior analytic terminology.
- Use slang in your writing.
- Submit work without proofreading.

Responding to Corrective Feedback on Assignments

As you progress in your educational journey, content and requirements may become more challenging. While you may be used to excelling in your courses, it's expected that you will encounter coursework with which you're not immediately fluent. Though it may be difficult to face a grade you regard as poor, it's important to shift your mindset and recognize that grades can serve as a form of performance feedback to help you identify areas in which you can still show growth.

It can be disappointing to receive corrective feedback or to receive a lower than anticipated grade despite your best efforts. If you disagree with corrective feedback or with your grade, you may respectfully reach out to your instructor for clarification. It may be a good idea to take time between receiving the feedback and reaching out to your instructor. A day to reflect may decrease emotional responding and help you formulate an email appropriate in tone and content. It is possible that, even though you believe you are correct, you may not be the best judge of your work at that moment. There may also be situations in which your instructor has mistakenly provided corrective feedback that was meant for someone else or may have made an error in grading. Regardless, you should take accountability for your grade; scores on assignments are earned rather than given. Further, assignments are crafted to assess various knowledge, skills, and abilities, and instructions and grading criteria are typically aligned with course competencies for the class as a whole. Your instructor most likely has not personally asked you to meet the criteria; instead, the assignment instructions require those criteria be present. No matter which situation you are in, you will have greater growth and facilitate a better relationship with your instructor if you thoughtfully craft your response with consideration for tone.

Example:

> Hi Professor Cleary,
> Thank you so much for your thoughtful feedback on my week 5 submission. I wanted to ask for clarification on the scoring for this submission. I see I lost points on my assignment because I did not provide examples and non-examples for my operational definition. I believe that I provided an example on page 3 and a non-example on page 4. Could you provide me with some guidance on how I could have improved those examples or how I could have better incorporated them?
> Thank you,
> Perry Student

Non-example:

> Why would you take points off of my assignment? I included everything you asked for in the instructions. I have always done well in all of my courses and will be reaching out to the Dean.

Example:

> Hi Professor Cleary,
> I'm reaching out regarding my week 2 assignment. I saw that I lost points for my submission being late. I had emailed you on Wednesday morning regarding an emergency and

requested an extra day to turn in my assignment and you approved that request. I have attached the message below. Thank you so much for your thoughtful feedback on my paper and your assistance with this matter!
Best,
Xi Student

Non-example:

I read in your feedback that i didn't turn my assignment in on time. I asked for a one day extension and you told me it was fine. Its very unfair that you would take the points off after you told me i could have an extra day.

Do:

- Take accountability for your work; points are earned, not given and taken from you.
- Contact your instructor to request support or clarification on feedback.
- If the instructor communication doesn't resolve your concern, reach out to an appropriate party, such as your academic advisor, a university representative, or the academic department supervisor.

Don't:

- Make it personal.
- Use argumentative language.
- Threaten your instructor.

Self-Reflection Station

1 Reflect on your current communication style with your instructors. Are you remaining professional and objective in the way that you communicate or do you let your emotions take over? Is there a strategy that you use or could start using to decrease emotional responding to help you keep a more professional tone in exchanges?

2   Consider your current routine for written assignments. Do you take the time to prepare for each assignment by studying the instructions and scoring guide first? Do you attempt to find answers to your questions within the materials that are provided before communicating with your instructor? Are there certain programs that you want to start using to check spelling and grammar?

Practice: How Would You Respond?

Compare your responses to our recommendations at the end of this book.

1   A peer posted something controversial in the courseroom discussion board and is using non-behavior analytic resources to support their statement. You see that multiple other students agree or are reading the resource provided to try to learn more about the content posted. You disagree with the initial post and are able to support your thoughts with published, peer-reviewed behavior analytic research. How would you respond to this peer in the courseroom discussion?
2   You are a student in an ABA course. You are unhappy with a score that you have been given on your latest assignment. After reviewing the feedback provided by the instructor stating that you were missing assignment components, you feel like you did provide the information required. According to your recalculation of your grade, you should earn 20 points back, which would bring your grade from a 70% to a 90%. How would you write your email correspondence to your instructor in this situation?

References

Aguilar-Roca, N., Williams, A., Warrior, R., & O'Dowd, D. (2009). Two minute training in class significantly increases the use of professional formatting in students to faculty email correspondence. *International Journal for the Scholarship of Teaching and Learning*, *3*(1), 1–15. doi:10.20429/ijsotl.2009.030115

Chen, H.-T. M., Horne, B. D., Florell, D., & Thomas, M. (2021). Effects of priming messages to decrease negativity in online learning environments. *Scholarship of Teaching and Learning in Psychology, 7*(4), 301–311. doi:10.1037/stl0000195

Galikyan, I., & Admiraal, W. (2019). Students' engagement in asynchronous online discussion: The relationship between cognitive presence, learner prominence, and academic performance. *The Internet and Higher Education, 43*, 1–9. doi:10.1016/j.iheduc.2019.100692

Kazemi, E., Rice, B., & Adzhyan, P. (2018). *Fieldwork and supervision for behavior analysts: A handbook.* Springer.

Luiselli, J. K. (Ed.). (2023). *Applied behavior analysis advanced guidebook: A manual for professional practice.* Elsevier.

Ondrusek, A. L. (2012). What the research reveals about graduate students' writing skills: A literature review. *Journal of Education for Library and Information Science, 53*(3), 176–188.

Rahman, K. M. R., Anwar, S., & Numan, S. (2008). Enhancing distant learning through email communication: A case of BOU. *Turkish Online Journal of Distance Education, 9*(2), 180–185.

3 Writing as a Clinician

Charissa Knihtila and Michelle Fuhr

As a behavior analyst delivering clinical services, your job requires written communication (Kazemi et al., 2018), both within and outside of sessions. Session documentation is a form of within-session written communication that ensures that all individuals on the case, including the supervisor and technicians, have the necessary information to implement proper services. This documentation helps you to stay organized and tracks details so they can be referenced by multiple parties, and it allows you to freeze an event in time so you can review the relevant details at a later date. Other types of documentation that take place outside of sessions include reports and summaries that are important for justifying services to funding sources, establishing behavioral baselines and selecting goals for intervention, and providing progress updates.

The specific format and type of documentation may vary according to funding sources, agency or company requirements, and state and local requirements. Be sure to familiarize yourself with the requirements for your specific situation. Regardless of other requirements, clinical documentation requires a careful balance of clear, accurate, and concise information along with compassionate delivery. Clinical documentation may be read by many parties, not all of whom are behavior analysts, so you will need to use accessible language. Remember that clients and/or their caregivers will likely read these documents, as well as supervisors and funding sources. Rarely, legal situations may arise where your documentation may be read by attorneys or other parties outside of the original team. It is exceptionally important that all documents related to clinical work, including within and outside of session

DOI: 10.4324/9781003463498-3

documents, are written in such a way that they can be shared with others as appropriate and with the correct permissions. Even your own notes are subject to examination by the client, caregivers, supervisors, funders, and, potentially, other people.

Assessments

When starting to work with a new client, the first step is to conduct an assessment to determine the behavior to target and the function of behavior, set goals, and select the interventions that will be most effective in reaching those goals. Assessments are also conducted at regular intervals during the course of intervention to determine if there should be changes in the treatment plan. Assessment may be made of behavioral excesses, current skill levels, environmental variables, and any other factors that may impact the need for intervention or the type of intervention selected. The number and type of assessments used will vary based on the specific requirements in your location (e.g., your state, the county within your state), funding source (e.g., state-funded, private pay, insurance), and setting (e.g., center-based, in-home program, school-based, or business setting).

Assessment outcomes are typically summarized in a formal report. Although you should always follow your specific workplace requirements, your writing should include common factors in each type of assessment. It is also common to combine different kinds of assessments into a single report. Your assessment report will likely include summaries of data from various sources, your interpretation of the data, and recommendations for actions to take based on the data. These recommendations may also include specific goals to be addressed as a result of the assessment.

Remember that the assessment report may be read by the individual being assessed or their caregivers, some of the people who work with the individual, and funding sources or other decision makers. Therefore, you should avoid using jargon and keep your language compassionate, clear, and to the point. Although the purpose of the assessment report is to report data and make recommendations for intervention, contextual information about the specific assessments should be included so that the reader is able to understand how the data were gathered.

Indirect Assessments

When conducting indirect assessments, you are usually obtaining information from other people. Sometimes, this takes the form of structured or unstructured interviews or surveys that can result in a lot of qualitative information that must be sorted and summarized. Retain your notes and transcripts as raw data, but it is helpful to consolidate similar types of information and remove anything that is not relevant to the assessment for your report. Choose the most important points to support a clear understanding of the needs of the individual you are assessing and provide specific examples. Be sure to identify the informant for the information that you have gathered and explain their relationship to the client.

Example:

> Antonio's teacher, Mr. DeShawn, reports that Antonio engages in hitting peers frequently throughout the school day, with the greatest frequency of hitting during math and reading activities and the least amount of hitting during recess and lunch.

Non-example:

> Antonio's teacher indicates that Antonio arrives to school on time most days and eats breakfast in the cafeteria. He has several friends. He does not always finish his breakfast. On arrival in the classroom the students do a morning circle time routine which can be loud and chaotic. Antonio's teacher also says that Antonio enjoys circle time. He reports that the class then transitions to language arts time followed by science, art, and math. He usually hits his friends during math but not science or art. After lunch the students then go to recess and return for reading. Sometimes he also hits during reading.

Sometimes, interviewees may use mentalistic language in their discussion of target behaviors (e.g., he hits because he is mad), but your summary of these interviews should use objective language. If interpretations or opinions are included, be sure to attribute those to the interviewee specifically, with no indication that you are providing your own opinions based on the interviewee responses.

Example:

> Andi's parents, Mr. Smith and Ms. Brown, state that they think that Andi cries because they are upset about screen time being over.

Non-example:

> Andi is crying because they are upset about losing their screen time.

Example:

> Mrs. Smith, Haley's teacher, reports that Haley engages in verbal protest by stating that she doesn't want to do her classwork in a loud voice, asking why she has to, complaining that it is too hard, or trying to change the topic of conversation during class independent work time to a preferred topic with both her teacher and peers. Mrs. Smith states this causes her to spend more time with Haley instead of being able to walk around the classroom and assist other students who are asking for help and that on occasion (2 or 3 times a week) other students join in Haley's "complaining."

Non-example:

> Haley's classroom work is too difficult for her and she is looking for help or to avoid it by using verbal protest and complaining about how she doesn't want to do it or it's too hard. She also likes it when she can convince her peers to complain too because then no one has to do the work at that time.

Descriptive Assessments

Descriptive assessment involves recording your own observations of behavior. All writing should be based on what you observed, followed by an analysis of the qualitative and quantitative data you collected. You should not include your opinions or assumptions when describing your observations. Writing should include only clear, concise, objective, observable, and measurable language. Sometimes, you will also use data collected by others as part of your direct assessment. Clearly identify how data were collected for descriptive assessments, including who collected the data, over what period of time data were collected, and any relevant environmental variables that occurred during data collection.

Similar to the data gathered for indirect assessment, you will need to summarize and analyze these data. Rarely do you report raw data in your assessment report. Rather, you may summarize descriptive data in a number of ways, depending on the purpose of the report and the requirements of the entity for whom you are writing. It may be appropriate to code the data and graph quantitative information. Alternatively, you may write a summary of the major themes that you see in the data. Such a written summary should be an objective description of the data collected, without analysis or assumptions about the meaning of the data.

Example:

> Ivy was observed engaging in verbal protest in the form of screaming profanities and specifically saying "No, I don't want to do that" 6 times in the 30 minute observation in the home setting.

Non-example:

> Ivy was angrily screaming profanities because she didn't want to engage in the task that was presented to her throughout the observation period.

Functional Analysis (FA)

When you conduct a systematic manipulation of environmental variables to confirm the hypothesized function of behavior, you are able to make the most informed analysis of behavior. There are many different types of functional analyses, but the results should be written with the same considerations for each.

As with indirect and descriptive assessments, data need to be described succinctly and without any assumptions by the assessor. You should clearly describe the procedures used in the functional analysis, being sure to illustrate attention paid to controlling variables as necessary, based on the type of experimental analysis. It is particularly important to describe functional analysis procedures without using jargon and with a compassionate tone, as the concept of functional analysis may be concerning to readers who are not familiar with experimental assessment. Highlight the safety precautions that are taken to mitigate the potential effects of reinforcing behavior during a functional analysis.

Example:

> Results of the latency-based functional analysis indicate that self-injurious behavior is likely maintained by attention. Conditions were 90 seconds in length and each was conducted 4 times. Self-injury occurred an average of 5 seconds after attention was removed, with a range of 3–8 seconds. During the escape condition, self-injury occurred an average of 80 seconds following the placement of a demand, with a range of 78–82 seconds. No instances of self-injury occurred in the control condition.

Non-example:

> Results of the experimental analysis indicate that the client wanted attention so they engaged in self-injury. Self-injury occurred most often during the attention condition with an occasional instance in the escape condition and no instances in the control condition.

Example:

> Results of the brief functional analysis show that aggressions are likely to be influenced by escape from demands. Conditions were 5 minutes in length and each was conducted 3 times. Aggressions were evoked an average of 6 times in the

presence of demands. Aggressions occurred at an average of 3 times in the attention condition. Aggressions were not evoked in the tangible and alone conditions.

Non-example:

Results of the brief functional analysis showed that the client had a hard time when demands were presented and engaged in aggressions. Aggressions occurred a few times in the attention condition as well.

Skills Assessment

A skills assessment is used to determine an individual's current skill levels across different domains. There are many different specific skills assessments with associated curricula, but you can write about each assessment in similar ways. A written summary of a skills assessment should present a balanced discussion that addresses areas of strength and need. It is important to remain positive in your tone even when discussing areas of concern.

When writing about skills assessment outcomes, provide some context by explaining the nature of the assessment. You may also describe how the assessment was normed, if relevant, and what is meant by norms, remembering that your client and/or their caregiver will also read this report. Explain how the assessment was conducted, including the setting, who was present during the assessment, and the duration of the assessment. For reports of skills assessments, you should provide a brief behavioral observation that notes qualitative data about how the individual responded to the demands of the assessment, what reinforcers were used to promote engagement, and if breaks were needed.

As most skills assessments span different domains or areas, it is common to follow a formula when reporting the outcomes of the assessment. First, introduce the domain, explaining what it means. Next, identify the individual's level of ability within the domain and, then, offer some examples to support the statements that you make about strengths and weaknesses.

Example:

> An [assessment name] was conducted with Mason on August 24, 2023 from 2–4 p.m. in his home setting with his grandmother, Suri, present. [Assessment name] is a criterion-referenced assessment that measures Mason's performance against set learning criteria and includes skills typically acquired by kindergarten. Mason initiated engagement and participated actively in assessment. He exhibited the ability to tact 50 pictures of common items independently and follow novel 2- and 3-step instructions independently. When asked to identify pictures based on feature, function, and class, Mason was able to identify 2 out of 25 trial opportunities. The two identified were features and related to color identification of a red and blue item. He demonstrated a preference for social praise as a form of reinforcement.

Non-example:

> Mason is able to tact enough pictures of common items and can follow simple instructions. Mason does not know how to identify pictures based on feature, function, or class even though he was able to identify two different colors.

Do:

- Use a template for reporting assessment results if one is provided.
- Write in clear, concise, and objective behavior analytic terminology.
- Summarize information gathered via interview or observation in objective and measurable language.
- Report only the data that were gathered or observed.
- Provide behavior analytic interpretations of the observations/conditions.
- Identify any people who provided information by name.

Don't:

- Provide your opinion related to interviews, observations, or data.

- Make and/or report assumptions based on the data collected during the assessment.
- Use casual language referring to an individual.
- Focus only on areas of need.

Interpretations in Assessment Reports

Analysis

After summarizing data collected from your assessments, you will write an analysis and recommendations. This is where you can provide your own opinion and hypotheses, but you must label them as such. Include a statement about the limitations of your analysis based on the information gathered. In your analysis, clearly state what you think the data mean and explain why. Avoid any language that implies assumptions about what the individual is thinking, feeling, or intends by their behavior. Your conclusions should be drawn from the data collected during your assessments that are shared in the report and not any other source of information.

Example:

> During a brief, 60-minute observation, it was observed that Reina engaged in hair pulling each time she was asked to "clean up" which resulted in caregivers providing reprimands including "no," "don't do that," and "stop," then assisting with cleaning up. It is hypothesized that the function of hair-pulling is escape from non-preferred activities. A functional analysis will be conducted to test this hypothesis. Although the caregivers reported that this was typical responding for Reina, the short length of the observation is a limitation and further assessments are warranted.

Non-example:

> Reina engages in hair-pulling to get her parents to complete her cleaning tasks for her.

Recommendations

Recommendations may include the initiation, continuation, titration, or discharge of various services. Depending on your role and the requirements of the entity for which you are writing, you may also need to recommend a dosage or intensity of services. It is helpful to accompany dosage recommendations with references to research, industry standards, or other credible sources.

You may also recommend specific interventions based on the outcomes of the assessment. While it is appropriate to use the correct terminology for interventions, you should also provide a brief description of the intervention for the benefit of non-behavior analyst readers. It is useful to reference literature that supports recommended interventions as evidence-based practices.

All recommendations should be based upon the analysis of the data from your assessments, so it is helpful to write clear guidance that shows how each recommendation relates to the conclusions drawn from the data you collected. Think of the recommendations as the final link in a chain that starts with data collection, proceeds to analysis, and results in actionable steps. Each recommendation should be supported by the data and analysis in the report.

Example:

> Based on observation and the results of the initial assessments, it is recommended that skill deficits and behavioral excesses be addressed through therapy based on applied behavior analysis, focusing on the social communication deficits of autism. Sara will benefit from an environment that is enriched with many learning opportunities to address socialization, self-management, and flexibility. It is recommended that a combination of discrete trial instruction (DTI) and natural environment teaching (NET) be included in the treatment. To achieve optimal progress and based on developmental needs, it is recommended Sara participate in our treatment for 10 total hours per week, across 3–4 times per week.

Non-example:

> It is recommended that Sara receive 10 hours of home-based ABA services to decrease challenging behaviors and improve skills.

Goals

Performing assessments usually leads to generating goals. As a behavior analyst, you are trained to choose goals based on the available information along with considerations including environmental and cultural variables as well as client preferences. Goals are usually delivered as written statements about expected or desired outcomes of behavioral interventions. Depending on the situation, you may be expected to produce long-term goals, short-term goals, or both.

Clarity is key in writing goals. Language must be accessible to the client and/or their caretaker, the people who are going to be implementing interventions to achieve the goals (i.e., technicians or teachers), and any other relevant party such as funders or program supervisors. Goals should identify behavior in measurable terms and state how much behavior change should be observed to consider the goal complete, and within what period of time.

Reduction goal example:

> Shelby will reduce hitting from a baseline of 15 occurrences per hour to zero instances of hitting across 3 consecutive weeks with 2 staff members and caregivers, in the home and community setting.

Reduction goal non-example:

> Shelby will stop hitting by three months of service.

Skill acquisition goal example:

> Jose will increase independent single-word manding from a baseline of 0% of opportunities to 80% of opportunities across 2 consecutive weeks with 2 staff members in the school setting and with caregivers in the home setting.

Non-example:

> Jose will be able to use single-word mands with caregivers and school staff at least 80% of the time.

Do:

- Keep a positive tone in your writing.
- Provide your opinion (labeled as your opinion) based on analysis of the assessment.
- Provide recommendations and goals with clear, concise, behavior analytic terminology.
- Write only measurable goals.
- Use the individual's name when appropriate versus "individual" or "client."
- Refer to caregivers/supporters by name, if referred to.

Don't:

- Focus only on areas of need.
- Use mentalistic terms in your goals.
- Use casual language referring to an individual.
- Editorialize or make assumptions based on your opinion.

Documentation of Services

Behavior analysts must document services in a variety of ways. Frequency and type of documentation vary depending on location and funding source. Your documentation is also important to you as a clinician because it summarizes the data that you use to make decisions in your practice. Documentation provides a historical record of the services provided, strategies implemented, and the level of effectiveness of interventions.

Just like assessments, documentation may be read by different people, including clients and/or their caregivers, funding sources, and people who work with the client. In some instances, documentation is required for legal reasons and may be subpoenaed or requested for release by clients. Documentation must always be up-to-date, accurate, and precise. As always, strive to use clear and comprehensible language, explaining any jargon.

Compassion in documentation means being clear, client-focused, honest, and balanced. It may be tempting to write for the desired outcome, such as "getting insurance to cover services" or "convincing a school district to recommend a certain placement," but your documentation must not be biased. Reporting accurately allows for all parties to make informed decisions in the best interests of the client.

Progress Reports

Requirements for progress reports vary based on funding source, setting, and location, but all include common features such as data reporting and discussion of progress related to each goal. Before reporting data and progress, however, it may be appropriate to provide some background information on the individual, including their diagnosis, a brief social history, current setting or level of services, and any significant changes in their life since the last progress report. Life changes may include changes in living situations, family configurations, health, or other variables.

After centering the individual as the focus of the report, you should summarize data collected from interventions and present them in an easily understood format for the audience. Progress reports often include graphs showing data over time. Be sure that any graphs included in a progress report are properly labeled and visually clear. Some things to look out for and correct are missing axis labels, cluttered data paths that are hard to follow because they overlap, and missing phase change lines or labels. Include a brief description of the data in written format as well so that a reader who is not fluent in reading graphs can still understand the meaning of the data.

In addition to presenting graphed data for goals, explain the status of each goal. Was it met, is it in progress, or was it discontinued? If a goal was not met, provide an update on the progress of that goal and any changes that were made to the plan since the last progress report. For example, you may need to explain if any changes were made to how the goal was measured, the intervention plan, or the definition of the target behavior. If these or other changes were made, reflect

Writing as a Clinician 43

those on the graph with a phase change line and label. Some progress reporting templates list goals in a table, with columns for data summaries and determination of progress. These tables can be very helpful for allowing the reader to see goal progress at a glance.

End your progress report with recommendations. You may make recommendations for services to start, continue, or terminate. You may also make recommendations for certain interventions based on the progress of current goals or the need for new goals. New goals might be recommended, especially if current or recent goals have been met. Keep your recommendations section organized by type of recommendation, usually moving from general to more specific. For example, it's common to start by recommending a certain level of service, then particular interventions, and then new goals. It is also appropriate to organize your recommendations by domain or area of focus. For example, you can group all recommendations related to community functioning together, and all recommendations for home priorities together.

Example:

> Hannah continues to progress through identifying objects based on feature, function, and class. Data show slow progression in this goal, but there is an increasing trend, specifically in the area of selecting by feature. The current targets in selecting by feature focus on colors and shapes. The goal will continue and targets will continue to be evaluated for relevance in Hannah's daily life.

Non-example:

> Hannah struggles with identifying objects based on feature, function, and class. There is a very slow upward trend, but only in selected by common features such as color and shape. The goal needs to be continued so that the client can learn this skill.

Example:

> Julie's current level of social skills is an area for improvement to strengthen learning opportunities and social interactions

with peers. Skills to address in this area include learning appropriate ways to obtain attention from peers, compromising when playing with peers, reciprocal conversations with peers, and appropriate requests to peers to stop unwanted actions. Baseline on these skills is currently below 20% of opportunities presented.

Non-example:

Julie's weak social skills make it difficult for peers to interact with her. Julie engages in aggressions and other inappropriate behaviors and goals to address this are needed.

Session Notes

Session notes are written by the person who is providing the direct service to the client or caregiver. As a behavior analyst, you may write session notes and you may train others to write them, including technicians, direct care staff, or classroom aides. Session notes can function as support that billable services occurred and must therefore meet billing expectations and consistency. You should avoid copying and pasting previous information into a new current note as this may resemble fraudulent activity if two identical or very similar notes are submitted. Instead, rewrite the note with new language to support that it was a new interaction.

Session notes may be written for various types of client interactions, such as direct contact hours performed by behavior technicians and overseen by behavior analysts; assessments and observations; team meetings; and interactions with caregivers, case managers, other professionals, and funding sources (e.g., insurance companies or school districts). While each of these notes varies in type of information documented, all session notes should include some consistent basic elements. Necessary client information will depend on the funding source requirements, but minimally includes the client's name and date of birth. Session notes also usually include a list of the people present at the session, including staff, caregivers, and any other family members. Depending on company policy and the nature of the session, you may also be asked to provide a billing code on the session note. The exact date and time of the session should be documented on the session note and must match any billing documents. The location of services should be noted, including if services were delivered by phone or telehealth.

In addition to noting these details, clinical documentation is also part of session notes. If the client was present for the session, a brief observation of the client should be documented. The observation may document the overall appearance of the client, such as clothing appropriate for the weather. The observation may also include relevant information about the environment (e.g., number of other children present and the ratio of students to paraprofessionals, or narrative ABC data on significant events that occurred during the session). You do not need to recreate the data collected as part of your session, but can make a general statement summarizing those data. It is best to write the notes in real time to avoid accidentally modifying details of the session, if company policy supports this strategy.

Additional clinical documentation may include consultation with others involved in the session, such as information received from caregivers or training and feedback provided to technicians or caregivers. Recommendations for further assessment or treatment modification can also be provided here. Finally, session notes may be used to document risks or concerns such as the occurrence of unsafe behavior, potential drawbacks of current interventions, or need for staff training and support.

A session note becomes part of the client's file and can be accessed by caregivers and audited by funding agencies. Because behavior technicians and caregivers are the primary implementers of behavior analysis services, it may be difficult for you to find the line between documenting client medical information and staff performance when completing a session note for a time when you provided supervision. Although staff performance may be commented on through the education and treatment updates provided, behavior analysts should remember that client session notes function primarily as documentation of services and are not intended for staff performance monitoring. Detailed notes of staff performance (e.g., concerns with adherence to treatment, retention of feedback, and implementation errors) should be documented separately to avoid staff information being maintained in the client's file.

The writing for session notes must be clear, complete, and professional, with no assumptions or emotional language. Compassion in writing your session notes is also important. While these notes are official documents, they are also available to the client and their caregivers to read. Avoid using jargon and adopt a tone that is professional but kind. Professional writing is essential for session notes. You may have to document uncomfortable situations and difficult conversations. It is important to stay honest and true to the events that took place during the session, but to document them in a professional manner, free of biases, judgment, or harsh language. Be especially mindful of tone when writing about sessions that were difficult or less productive. Highlight positive things that happen in sessions in addition to recording concerning events. Sharing the clinical notes with clients and/or caretakers at the end of the session helps to maintain open, professional communication, even during challenging sessions.

Example:

> Kai screamed and slammed the door shut when asked to transition away from his game upon RBT arrival. He was reassured that he could pause his game and play more during breaks, which helped the transition. He had a great time blowing bubbles in the yard during the manding program and didn't want to return to his game after that.

Non-example:

> Kai was mad when I arrived because he wanted to play his game. I told him he could earn his game but then he didn't even want it after a while.

Example:

> Sonia engaged in high rates of aggression toward me throughout the session. Not many skill programs were run. Instead, I focused on behavior management programs and prompting the identified calming strategies when aggression occurred. By the time the session ended, Sonia was using strategies independently, and I conducted some manding trials.

Non-example:

> Sonia was extremely aggressive and attacked everyone all session today. We got nothing done and I couldn't run any programs except at the very end.

Example:

> Today's session was a little hectic. There were extra people in the home due to family visiting from out of town. Brady had a hard time focusing on his more difficult skills, following three-step instructions and independent leisure skills, due to the extra noise. I discussed the situation with his mom and we agreed that today would be a great day to focus on socializing with Brady's cousins who were visiting. Brady needed some prompting with turn taking and sharing his toys, but did great practicing his conversation skills today!

Non-example:

> Today's session was impossible. There were people everywhere and they were all being incredibly loud and distracting. I talked with Brady's mom and she said that today may not be a good day to work on some of his skills because he was excited to see his cousins. So, I had to abandon the treatment plan and we played with his cousins instead. He didn't share his things well, but did talk to his cousins.

Caregiver Session Notes

When caregivers receive "parent training" services or have other contact with behavior analysts, such as consultations, these interactions should be documented using a session note. Professional language should be balanced with caregiver-friendly, non-technical, and compassionate language that the caregiver will easily comprehend and won't find offensive. Note that, while "parent training" is the term typically used by funding sources, we advocate for more supportive, inclusive language when describing these services, such as "caregiver support" or "caregiver collaboration."

Similar to other types of notes, the caregiver note includes the basic elements documenting the client's identifying information, the caregiver's name, who was present during the session, and where the session was held. A clinical section describing the contents of the session should cover a variety of content depending on the nature of the session. For example, during a traditional parent training session, you would document the strategies used to teach the parent, the goals and targets of the session, and a summary of the parent's participation. You may also document the need to adjust strategies, goals, or other elements of the parent training plan.

Caregiver satisfaction is an area that should be commented on during the caregiver meetings and documented in notes. Having a separate heading for this topic functions as a prompt for the behavior analyst to inquire about caregivers' perspectives of treatment goals, procedures, and results of the current intervention. Inquiring about caregiver satisfaction can lead to conversations on improving treatment, and including caregiver input in the treatment plan. Some funding sources may require documentation of caregiver satisfaction.

Example:

> I met with Sam's parent, Alex, for caregiver collaboration. We practiced gathering data on the frequency of manding and the reinforcement procedures outlined in the behavior plan. Alex actively participated and asked engaging questions and sought support throughout. When asked about his current comfort level with the plan, he indicated support for the procedures and a desire to focus caregiver collaboration sessions on antecedent strategies to promote more spontaneous communication.

Non-example:

> Dad participated in parent training and was unable to accurately record data on manding throughout the session. He required frequent prompting to refrain from delivering the iPad when Sam whined for it.

Do:

- Use a template if one is provided.
- Be clear and complete in your documentation.
- Report progress for each goal as met, in progress, or discontinued.
- Provide a visual display of data to allow for visual analysis of results.
- Provide an explanation with the visual display related to progress reported.
- Write honestly, but with a professional tone.
- Use objective, but compassionate, language when detailing the session.
- Use the individual's name when appropriate versus "individual" or "client."
- Refer to caregivers/supporters by name rather than "mom" or "dad."

Don't:

- Use harsh language.
- Use a judgmental or biased tone.
- Skip discussion of any goals.
- Focus only on what went "wrong" during the session or reporting period.
- Provide your opinion, editorialize, make inferences or assumptions, or use mentalistic language.
- Use casual language referring to an individual (e.g., "kiddo").

Self-Reflection Station

1   As clinicians, our goal is to provide documentation that demonstrates what we did for the purposes of adequate record keeping and reimbursement. However, "charting" or "documentation time" can feel like a secondary activity. How can you make documentation of your activities a priority in your schedule to make sure you are adequately documenting your work?

2 It is common for clinical programs to have "goal banks" to improve efficiency for clinicians activating new curricula or goals for a consumer. However, these banks are boilerplate templates that are not individualized. Honestly reflect on times that you have copied and pasted goals from one client to another and how it went. Did the client make adequate progress quickly, or would more individualization have been helpful?

Practice: How Would You Respond?

Compare your responses to our recommendations at the end of this book.

1 As the clinical director of an ABA organization, you review supervision notes from an early career clinician, Ally, and notice inconsistencies that raise concerns about potential billing inaccuracies. These inconsistencies include discrepancies between service descriptions and billed hours, as well as instances of duplicated content. When you meet with Ally, you kindly explain that she does not fully know how to write a quality session note and is using poor examples as guides. What are three or four recommendations you could give to Ally on how to improve her overall documentation?
2 Imagine sitting down with a family to delve into the reasons behind their child's tendency to hit or attempt to hit. According to the parents, hitting is due to an anger management problem. What are three open-ended questions you could ask to gain more information regarding hitting and further assess the function of the behavior?

Reference

Kazemi, E., Rice, B., & Adzhyan, P. (2018). *Fieldwork and supervision for behavior analysts: A handbook*. Springer.

4 Writing as a Leader

Danielle Bratton and Dana Reinecke

Communicating with Caregivers

Compassion-Focused Communication

Raising children is no simple task, and caregivers are faced with sometimes excessive input from well-meaning family members, doctors, specialists, therapy providers, social media, and countless strangers with unsolicited advice. Even if unsolicited advice is offered with the best of intentions, imagine the toll this must take on anyone, let alone the caregiver of an individual who requires additional support.

Behavior analysts write to caregivers regularly (see Chapter 3, Writing as a Clinician). It's important to keep written records not only to document training for funders and as a record of the instructions given, but also to ensure the family has clear guidance to which they can refer at any time in the future. They can be protective for behavior analysts in terms of liability, but also a powerful resource to a family dealing with information overload. To ensure you masterfully accomplish these tasks, it is important to develop exceptional written communication with caregivers.

Before considering the content of any message, we must develop the skill of compassion, which combines empathy with action. Empathy, or the ability to adopt a different person's perspective (Sivaraman, 2017), is a common skill targeted for individuals with social communication deficits, but do we use this skill ourselves in our interactions with others? When we fail to first consider how our caregivers may perceive feedback, we risk damaging our relationship and harming their personal welfare. With empathy as the

DOI: 10.4324/9781003463498-4

foundation of caregiver communication, the content of a message can be developed more effectively, demonstrating compassion. While in face-to-face meetings with caregivers, your words can be moderated by body language, facial expressions, and tone, but your written communication has to speak for itself. The feedback, information, and advice you provide result in a permanent product which may be controlled by others. You have an opportunity to leave a positive and lasting impact on families with skillful employment of empathic written communication.

There are several ways that you can demonstrate compassion in your writing to caregivers. First, be thoughtful in your word choice. Using "we" instead of "you" helps to show the caregiver that they are not alone in receiving feedback or working on goals, but rather that you are on a team with them. Similarly, use team language rather than divisive language to facilitate teamwork rather than competition. At times, you will not be the only professional working with the family and may need to coordinate with school or other providers. You may need to write about the work being done by others and should avoid "us versus them" language. It is also a good idea to be mindful of using jargon with caregivers. Some caregivers may prefer technical terminology, but others may find it unpleasant or overwhelming. Assess caregivers' preferences for terminology, and, if the caregiver is new to terminology, it's always a good idea to pair jargon with definitions or examples.

Next, describe the things you and the caregiver want to see rather than the things you don't want to see, to keep a positive tone in the communication. Keeping the focus on positive behavior change and growth rather than decreasing problem behavior is helpful in approaching behavior change from the most functional, effective, and compassionate stance. Finally, acknowledge the caregiver's role and provide behavior-specific praise to emphasize their importance. Noting caregiver input into goals or interventions and how caregivers have contributed to their child's success sets a positive tone and makes connecting with you reinforcing.

Team language example:

> We can show Kareem that he can get our attention by asking for help.

Team language non-example:

> You should show Kareem that he can get your attention by asking for help.

Team language example:

> The school has stated that concerning behaviors have increased this past week. When Carmine gets upset, the team is trying to assist by allowing him cool-down time outside of the classroom. We can schedule a meeting to share strategies and data to come up with a solution which is best for Carmine.

Team language non-example:

> The school has stated that concerning behaviors have increased this past week. They've been allowing Carmine to leave the classroom when he gets upset which is reinforcing his behavior. We need to meet with the school to discuss their approach and what they should do instead.

Limiting jargon example:

> Today we discussed the use of timers for decreasing Alec's cursing behavior. You will remind Alec that if he can use his nice words for 2 minutes, he can earn his token. Set your timer for 2-minutes and give Alec his token when the timer beeps if he did not curse.

Limiting jargon non-example:

> Today we discussed using a DRO procedure with Alec. Be sure reinforcement delivery is contingent on the absence of cursing.

Focus on growth example:

> We can work together to teach Alejandro to request the tablet using his picture icon. When he screams, we can prompt him to use his picture icon to ask for the tablet instead.

Focus on growth non-example:

> You should stop giving Alejandro the tablet when he screams. You are providing him with the item he wants for the wrong behavior.

Including caregiver input example:

> Thank you so much for your active involvement in planning and helping us keep Latrice's best interests as the primary focus. Your input is invaluable. I agree that knowing the alphabet is going to be a skill which helps Latrice in many aspects of her life. Let's talk about how we can get there. If we start by teaching Latrice to communicate her wants and needs …

Including caregiver input non-example:

> I'm going to introduce a manding program for Latrice because these skills are more important than teaching her the alphabet at this time. She needs to be able to communicate her wants and needs first.

Performance Feedback and Recommendations

It's common for behavior analysts to provide feedback to caregivers in written form. This may be part of a telehealth service, team notes, or documents to funders. Perhaps you're writing performance feedback on a session note following caregiver collaboration, a caregiver needs additional support from team members to consistently implement a treatment plan, or you need to document that a caregiver has not followed specific treatment recommendations. These types of written communication should adhere to the thoughtful writing guidelines described earlier, regardless of the intended audience and purpose of documentation. Remember that these are permanent products and reflect on us as behavior analysts and the field as a whole.

A good strategy for providing feedback to caregivers is to pair with reinforcement in the opening. Reminding the caregiver what they have done correctly may help them to be receptive to constructive feedback later on. This is also a good time to remember that reinforcement differs for everyone, even caregivers. Some caregivers may really appreciate hearing about what they did well, and some may find it more motivating to hear something positive about their child. Be specific and respectful in your praise, as it's much more meaningful to hear exactly what went well and why, rather than a generic "great job."

Constructive feedback should also be specific and include an objective goal or expectation. Identify exactly what needs to be done and how often or how much. When providing constructive feedback, consider what barriers may have prevented a caregiver from following a plan. Ideally, you should explore this with them prior to writing your feedback, and can refer back to a conversation where they agreed to a specific level of engagement.

Example:

> Good afternoon, Sherry. It's amazing how seamlessly you've been able to implement Morgan's picture schedule into your routine, that's no simple task! Now we're in a great position to focus heavily on building up his communication and vocabulary. Let's work on presenting Morgan with opportunities to request by having him vocally ask for his snack items.

Non-example:

> Good afternoon, Sherry. Be sure to require Morgan to request vocally for his snack instead of just handing it to him. Remember, we want to increase his communication and vocabulary!

Example:

> Thank you so much for your invaluable input. This ensures we can provide Fatima with the most effective treatment plan to help her quickly get her needs met in safe ways. Let's plan to have the ABC checklist used once a day this week and we can review what you saw when we meet on Friday!

Non-example:

> Just a reminder, data need to be collected regularly.

Example:

> Thank you for letting me know about the unplanned challenges you faced this week. I understand you have many competing demands, and not being able to put in the same level of effort on a weekly basis is part of life for everyone. You are doing the best you can and we can see how helpful you have been towards Toby's progress. How can I help reduce some barriers for you this week?

Non-example:

> Treatment integrity this week is not looking as good as last week's. Let's review what you need to do to implement the procedures we agreed on to help Toby.

Follow-Up Documentation

Follow-up documentation provides an opportunity for you to clearly and concisely communicate with caregivers about what was discussed during a meeting or session. These notes can serve as effective prompts to engage in some targeted behavior, documentation of recurring concerns or issues, or a means to keep multiple caregivers current on the program when they are unable to be present at the same time. Documentation also helps clarify what was discussed and avoid any misunderstandings about guidance or plans you have provided. This form of communication absolutely should not be used to threaten or intimidate caregivers.

If it is necessary to document a problem, the issue should first be discussed with the caregiver in conversation, with written follow-up including a review of that conversation. Some organizations require that the caregiver sign follow-up documentation as a way of ensuring that they are aware of and have access to the documents. Even if you are not required to get a signature on follow-up documentation, it is a good idea to show documentation to the caregiver and ask them to read it and let you know if anything needs to be clarified or if they disagree with anything you have written.

Example:

> We discussed the importance of collecting data as it relates to continuation of services, and I understand that it's still a challenge to complete. We tried a few things, but we haven't hit on a successful strategy yet. What else can I do to offer support? I'm mindful that the funding source might not continue to cover services if we don't document them properly, and caregiver data is a big piece of that.

Non-example:

> You were instructed to provide data, but for the second time this did not occur and you were informed that failure to do so might result in termination of services.

Do:

- Pair with reinforcement in the opening.
- Provide an overview of the goal, expectation, topic discussed, or situation as you understand it.
- Identify an area for development and state this in measurable terms as a skill to build (practice ___, increase ___, try ___).
- Document specific caregiver questions and concerns and clearly reiterate responses. Invite feedback and questions.

Don't:

- Focus only on what went wrong.
- Overwhelm the caregiver with multiple areas to improve or a lengthy message.
- Select language that suggests failure (you used the wrong ___, it's incorrect to ___, you need to stop ___).
- Include irrelevant details.
- Overcommit in writing.
- Use follow-up documentation as a threat.

Communicating with Non-Behavioral Colleagues or Team Members

Behavior analysts often work as members of interdisciplinary teams, and our communication will differ with other professionals who are not behavior analysts. While the nature of the conversation is more focused on technical details than conversations with caregivers, there is still limited room for behavioral jargon and a need to adhere to ethical guidelines while being sensitive to the roles and practices of those non-behavioral colleagues. We can use diplomatic and respectful communication with colleagues to facilitate an effective, comfortable team environment.

Writing for non-behavioral colleagues may occur in several ways, including email exchanges, team notes, consultation reports, and clinical documentation. The way you approach these permanent products can have a profound impact on your relationships with other professionals and, by extension, reflect on the field of behavior analysis as a whole. It is crucial to recognize that your written communication is not just a means to convey information; it is an opportunity to embody the qualities that define compassionate behavior analysts. When you approach these written interactions with your most collegial, compassionate, friendly, and professional voice, you not only nurture a positive rapport with your colleagues but also contribute to the broader perception of our field. Your words and tone can demonstrate our commitment to collaboration, empathy, and ethical conduct. They can showcase our dedication to understanding and addressing complex behavioral issues with a humanistic and person-centered approach. In essence, your written communication is a reflection of our collective values and principles, reinforcing the idea that behavior analysts are not just experts in their field but also compassionate professionals who genuinely care about the well-being of those they serve.

As always, be thoughtful in language choices, no matter what kind of writing you are doing. One important way to do this with colleagues is to use team language, rather than divisive wording. This choice helps to facilitate teamwork rather than competition. Using words such as "we," "together we can," and "our contributions in this plan" instead of "you," "your role," and "my plan" can have a big impact on the tone of your writing.

An issue that may come up in communicating with non-behavioral colleagues is how to address suggestions that may not be aligned with evidence-based practices in ABA. As behavior analysts are prohibited by our ethics code from practicing outside of our scope of training and from using non-evidence-based practices, this can be a very tricky situation to navigate with diplomacy. We recommend that you acknowledge the recommendation, state your limitations, and offer a contribution that is as closely aligned with the recommendation as possible while remaining ethical. Above all, avoid presenting as arrogant or dismissive of other disciplines as this will undoubtedly create tension within the team and potentially present a barrier to treatment.

Team language example:

> We have seen increases in problem behavior during a variety of different activities. There appears to be brief escalations during morning work, speech, and math. We've also noticed fewer escalations when preferred items and schedules are used. When do you find that Adam is most comfortable and engaged with what you are asking him to do?

Team language non-example:

> You have seen an increase in problem behavior during your sessions, but the ABA staff have not. What are you doing differently that is causing Adam to have behavior problems?

Addressing limitations example:

> I agree that Diana benefits from frequent breaks. While the ABA team will not be able to implement sensory integration therapy as it is outside of our area of practice, we could contribute by conducting an assessment on the function of the problem behavior so that we can incorporate all preferred activities into our sessions.

Addressing limitations non-example:

> Sensory integration therapy is not an evidence-based practice and it would be unethical for me to use it. ABA practices are more effective and can address the same issues.

Do:

- Pair with reinforcement in the opening.
- Provide a brief overview of the situation or discussion.
- Briefly describe your role, positions, restrictions, and so on.
- Use "team" language.
- Keep the communication client-centered.
- Keep the communication focused on achieving team goals, within your scope.
- Be solution-focused.

Don't:

- Dismiss or ignore ideas from team members.
- Tell any team members they are wrong.
- Use behavioral jargon in communication.
- Speak negatively about other professional areas of service.

Communicating with Policy Makers

Behavior analysis is sometimes seen as a relatively new field, even though the practices are based on scientific principles established over 100 years ago, leading to thousands of studies over decades of research. This perception may partly be due to relatively recent public policy efforts to regulate the practice of behavior analysis. Some of these efforts may include establishing state licensure for behavior analysts (Dorsey et al., 2009), adjusting the regulations around state licensure, and defining positions for behavior analysts in public domains such as schools, hospitals, or other human service settings. As these policies directly affect behavior analysts' ability to work and may at times reflect misunderstanding of the field, behavior analysts may want or even need to enter into communication with policy makers (Coop et al., 2023).

Such communication can take place in person, such as meeting with representatives or policy makers or attending lobbying events. In these situations, it may be a good idea to leave written materials with your audience so that your important points are easily available to them after your meeting ends. You may also call policy makers to share your thoughts or requests, and, under those circumstances, it can be helpful to prepare a written script for yourself so that you are able to make your points succinctly and clearly. Finally, written documents such as letters, petitions, or press releases can be important in public policy efforts.

Any written documentation created to support advocacy for behavior analysis will become permanent products that reflect upon the field and may be read by people who are not familiar with – or who are even adamantly opposed to – behavior analysis. It is therefore really important to be very mindful of the messaging, tone, and accuracy of what is written and shared. Behavior analysis suffers from a public relations problem that is frequently discussed within the field, along with ways to correct that problem (Callahan et al., 2019; Freedman, 2016; Smith, 2016). Following are some suggestions for approaching written communication with policy makers as a means of correcting misunderstandings and improving the public image of behavior analysis.

Know the Problem

When engaging in public policy advocacy or lobbying efforts, it is essential that you understand what you are asking for and why you are asking for it. Tempting as it may be to sign a petition or fire off a letter at the request of a trusted colleague or group, your support will be much more meaningful when you have a complete picture of the issues involved. This will allow you to clearly convey the problem and suggested solution, without including unnecessary and potentially distracting information. Remember that policy makers receive extraordinarily large numbers of requests per day for attention to matters that are just as important to others as your matter is to you. Your outreach is one of many in a pile, so, if it is not easy to read and understand and is cluttered with excessive information, your letter may not be attended to.

Part of the problem that you are trying to address may have to do with misconceptions about behavior analysis. Professionals from other fields may raise concerns about behavior analysis in public policy and mount protests against licensing behavior analysts or access to behavior analysis in certain settings. These protests are usually based on misunderstandings, which you may wish to refute in your messaging to the policy makers. When addressing misunderstandings, it's helpful to first acknowledge that there is often little public awareness of behavior analysis (Freedman, 2016). We are great at communicating with each other through journals and conferences, but behavior analysis does not often show up in popular media outlets. It is therefore not reasonable or helpful to be defensive about misunderstandings; we should rather take a friendly and educational approach in making such corrections.

Know Your Audience

Policy makers are not necessarily behavior analysts or consumers of behavior analytic services. It is best to assume that they are completely unfamiliar with behavior analysis and the issue that you are raising, unless you have some concrete information otherwise. When providing background information about behavior analysis to this audience, it is best to avoid jargon. Certain behavior analytic terms may be perceived by the general public as very unpleasant (Critchfield et al., 2017) and can create a barrier between you and your audience. Although, as a behavior analyst, you have been taught to use the correct terminology in your work, you have also been taught to consider the impact of your verbal behavior on a listener. Freedman (2016) suggests that behavior analysts undertake a re-branding effort that preserves scientific principles while creating greater accessibility and appeal for the public. Think about the message that you want policy makers to hear and carefully consider if any of the words you are using to convey that message would be likely to be misunderstood.

One exercise that can help in editing your word choices is to think about explaining the same concepts to a friend or family member who is not a behavior analyst. Think about what you want them to know about the concept and whether it is really important for them to know the terminology to receive your message. You can also think about how you prefer to receive information from professionals in your life who have specialized knowledge. Does it help or hurt when a doctor or dentist uses vocabulary that is unfamiliar to you? Do you want your mechanic to explain what is wrong with your car in lay terms (and dollars and cents) or do you really want to know the specific names for every part and process that needs attention?

Another consideration is whether your audience is more receptive to quantitative or qualitative data. Behavior analysts are trained to evaluate quantitative data and to demonstrate effectiveness through graphical displays of behavior change. It is absolutely important to use objective data when making decisions about interventions, but in certain circumstances it is worth remembering that your audience may not have the same background in data analysis. As phrased by Freedman (2016, p. 94), we may do well to play up the "warm and fuzzy" side of behavior analysis, especially when talking about outcomes. Stating that an individual's self-injury was reduced to 10% of baseline levels is very meaningful. Stating that a child was able to return to his home school to be educated among his neighbors and friends because his health and personal safety had improved significantly may be more powerful to some audiences, however.

One way to present behavior analysis in a new, more flattering light is to highlight what is new and different in the field. Many of the misconceptions about modern ABA come from unfortunate truths from the past. You should not deny that history, but rather use the current climate of trauma-informed, compassionate practices to reframe and revise perceptions about behavior analysis. Smith (2016) suggests lifting up how behavior analysis works in interesting and novel ways, including outside of the fields where it is most associated (i.e., interventions in autism and other disabilities). Showing how effective behavior analytic applications can be in other areas, such as health and wellness, can help to make behavior analysis more relatable. Identifying more mainstream behavior analytic interventions also helps to separate the current practice from prior, potentially problematic, practices.

Make Comparisons

Behavior analysis can also be made more relatable by using comparisons to other fields. Framing behavior analytic interventions within a medical or educational setting may increase confidence and trust. Furthermore, showing how public policy affecting behavior analysts may be similar or different from such policies for other professions can be very helpful. For example, it may be helpful to draw parallels between the practice of behavior analysis and the practice of psychology or mental health counseling for the purposes of discussing state licensure.

Another comparison that may be helpful in some circumstances is to show how behavior analysis is regulated in other, similar settings. This may be meaningful at the level of the service setting or even the state. For example, school policies might be influenced when administrators are shown how behavior analysts are able to be compensated within state-regulated agencies. Similarly, state licensing authorities might be open to developing licensing regulations for behavior analysts based on those used in neighboring states.

Elevate the Right Voices

Above all else, public policy efforts for behavior analysis are best supported by the consumer point of view. Although behavior analysts can and should enter into communication with representatives, lawmakers, and administrators on behalf of the field, it is often the voices of those receiving the services of behavior analysts who will have the most impact. This is rightfully so, as it is the consumers who are helped or harmed by behavior analysts. As a behavior analyst working on public policy efforts, you should solicit the consumer perspective to guide your focus and how you communicate about the field. When possible and when invited to do so, stand with consumers as they advocate for themselves.

Do:

- Highlight the voices of clients of ABA.
- Prepare written materials for potential use.
- Use a positive and friendly tone, with accessible language.

- Ensure the accuracy of your materials and statements.
- Know what you are asking for and why.
- Focus on socially significant results.
- Acknowledge the controversial history of ABA and present current compassionate and ethical practices.

Don't:

- Overcomplicate your message.
- Use behavioral jargon in written or spoken communication.
- Be defensive, especially when ABA as a treatment is challenged.
- Focus only on quantitative data.
- Deny or ignore the history of application of ABA.

Communicating with Funders and Medical Providers

In addition to engaging with policy makers, behavior analysts often find themselves advocating for the services they provide to clients when seeking funding or cooperation from medical providers. Funders may include insurance companies, community programs, government organizations, or any groups who could benefit from behavior analysis. Medical providers may also be involved in ensuring funding is allocated to the provision of behavior analytic services to those in need, and these providers may include diagnosing physicians, psychiatrists, or other doctors. Tailoring your message to address these stakeholders is crucial to ensure that appropriate services can be available to those in need.

Understanding Unique Needs

Before approaching medical professionals and funders, it is vital for behavior analysts to have an extensive knowledge of the beneficiaries and their background, skills, and needs. This information allows for careful consideration of what details should be included. Having a thorough understanding of what is and is not included in their plans, and the processes by which to request, amend, and appeal authorization decisions on behalf of the consumer as a provider, is paramount.

Outcome Projections

When communicating with funders and medical providers, you should project the potential outcomes of the proposed services. Use data to demonstrate how behavior analysis can positively impact the population or beneficiary. Illustrate how these services can lead to increased independence, improved quality of life, and reduced reliance on more costly interventions or institutional care. Projections should be grounded in reality and not overwhelmingly optimistic or pessimistic. An individual with limited skill development is not likely to begin complex calculus in six months' time. Similarly, an individual with more complex skill development is not likely to lose a majority of skills if the extraneous "wants" from your authorization (e.g., 30% supervision as opposed to the 20% that is standard) are not honored. Set realistic and achievable goals under the assumption that most of those goals can be met in the authorization period.

Customizing Proposals

Funders and medical providers need to see that behavior analysts are not offering generic solutions but rather providing services that offer a return on investment to all stakeholders. Tailor your proposals to align with the specific needs of those you are advocating for. Present concrete data and examples that demonstrate how the proposed services directly address challenges and objectives. Make it clear that the requested funding is essential to meet these specific needs and how funding and resources will be allocated. That means not simply copying and pasting goals directly from an assessment or goal bank. Instead, focus on the curriculum first, identifying the response class intended to be taught and determining prerequisite skills, the scope and sequence of skills required, and ways in which you will establish generative learning.

Evidence-Based Support

Use empirical evidence to support your proposal. Gather data that illustrate how behavior analysis can address the population or beneficiary. Present research findings that demonstrate how this approach has resulted in positive outcomes for invested parties. Make sure to provide adequate citations of sources in your writing and use that support to underlie the empirical nature of what you are proposing.

Accessibility and Inclusivity

Emphasize the importance of ensuring that the needs of those served are addressed in an inclusive and accessible manner. Advocate for policies and practices that guarantee equal access to services and treatment options. Make it clear that the requested funding or cooperation is not only about providing services but also about upholding the right to inclusive and equitable care.

Patient-Centered Approaches

Highlight the voices and preferences of those served in all communications. Medical professionals and funders should understand that the proposed services are client-centered, meaning they prioritize the individual's choices, values, and goals.

Do:

- Ensure you have knowledge in all areas related to funding and medical needs for the client before initiating communication.
- Project results that are grounded in reality.
- Use data to show support for the use of behavior analytic services.
- Ensure that the plan being presented is individualized and appropriate for the client.
- Provide scholarly resources to support your suggestions.
- Highlight the voices and preferences of the client.

Don't:

- Project overly optimistic or pessimistic results.
- Make promises or guarantees for specific results.
- Copy and paste generic goals.
- State that behavior analytic services are the only option.

Self-Reflection Station

1 Consider your current attitudes toward caregiver training. Do you find that it is an important and useful exercise, or is it something that takes time away from other responsibilities you have? Do you find yourself wishing it was not part of your clinical expectations? Try and describe what is causing these reactions. How can you overcome any obstacles to making caregiver training a priority in your practice?
2 Consider your attitudes toward interdisciplinary collaboration. Do you find that it is important and useful, or is it something that takes time away from other responsibilities you have? Do you find yourself wishing it was not part of your clinical expectations? Try and describe what is causing these reactions. How can you overcome any obstacles to participating effectively in interdisciplinary collaboration?

Practice: How Would You Respond?

Compare your responses to our recommendations at the end of this book.

1 You are working with an occupational therapist who is asking you to include a brushing and joint compression intervention throughout the client's day in order to reduce disruptive behavior. You are uncomfortable with the idea of implementing the procedure as it is not evidenced-based and are concerned about the issues that may arise with respect to billing services. How would you respond to the other individual in a professional way to express your concerns?
2 Before attending an interdisciplinary hearing, you are informed that the other professionals have expressed concern about your participation. They report that you are dismissive of their concerns and ideas and insist that only your interventions can be effective. Draft a short response to the team, asking for feedback on how you can improve your collaboration.

References

Callahan, K., Foxx, R. M., Swierczynski, A., Aerts, X., Mehta, S., McComb, M. E., Nichols, S. M., Segal, G., Donald, A., & Sharma, R. (2019). Behavioral artistry: Examining the relationship between the interpersonal skills and effective practice repertoires of applied behavior analysis practitioners. *Journal of Autism and Developmental Disorders*, *49*, 3557–3570. doi:10.1007/s10803-019-04082-1

Coop, B., Ice, E. D., Tomei, A., & Urbano Powell, R. (2023). Why public policy matters: A call to action for the everyday behavior analyst. *Behavior Analysis in Practice*. doi:10.1007/s40617-023-00878-x

Critchfield, T. S., Doepke, K. J., Kimberly Epting, L., Becirevic, A., Reed, D. D., Fienup, D. M., Kremsreiter, J. L., & Ecott, C. L. (2017). Normative emotional responses to behavior analysis jargon or how not to use words to win friends and influence people. *Behavior Analysis in Practice*, *10*, 97–106. doi:10.1007/s40617-016-0161-9

Dorsey, M. F., Weinberg, M., Zane, T., & Guidi, M. M. (2009). The case for licensure of applied behavior analysts. *Behavior Analysis in Practice*, *2*, 53–58. doi:10.1007/bf03391738

Freedman, D. H. (2016). Improving public perception of behavior analysis. *The Behavior Analyst*, *39*(1), 89–95. doi:10.1007/s40614-015-0045-2

Sivaraman, M. (2017). Using multiple exemplar training to teach empathy skills to children with autism. *Behavior Analysis in Practice*, *10*(4), 337–346. doi:10.1007/s40617-017-0183-y

Smith, J. M. (2016). Strategies to position behavior analysis as the contemporary science of what works in behavior change. *The Behavior Analyst*, *39*, 75–87. doi:10.1007/s40614-015-0044-3

5 Writing as a Supervisor

Celia Heyman and Renee Wozniak

Supervision by behavior analysts occurs in different contexts. Perhaps the most formal level of supervision is as an intervention for shaping the repertoire of an aspiring behavior analyst (Sellers et al., 2016; Turner et al., 2016) through ongoing interaction between the supervisor and the supervisee. Other types of supervision relationships managed by behavior analysts include overseeing the work of behavior technicians or paraprofessionals who might not be seeking further credentialing, or training and monitoring staff in an organizational setting.

Regardless of the type of supervision being provided, supervisors need to communicate effectively to provide models and feedback for their supervisees. Communication may include in vivo, remote, and written modalities. As a supervisor, you will need to create many written permanent products during the supervision relationship. If supervision occurs in the context of obtaining or maintaining a particular credential, it is important to follow the documentation guidelines of that credentialing organization. The permanent products commonly created by supervisors include supervision contracts, meeting documentation, evaluations and feedback, structured behavior analytic content, and documents for evaluating the effectiveness of supervision.

All written products related to supervision must be technological, informative, and culturally responsive. Written communication that is technological provides clear descriptions and is void of subjective interpretations to the greatest extent possible. An informative written product can influence the behavior of a supervisee in positive ways. Written communication that is culturally responsive reduces barriers

DOI: 10.4324/9781003463498-5

for supervisees to learn and acquire skills. For example, you might adjust requirements, expectations, and methods to address intersectionality of your supervisee's cultural variables and help them create a plan for ongoing assessment of their own biases (Beaulieu & Jimenez-Gomez, 2022).

Structured Behavior Analytic Content

Quality supervision is focused on the acquisition and maintenance of competencies for both knowledge-based and performance-based repertoires. It is vital for the supervisor to share systematic, structured content to assess, teach, and measure the progress of the supervisee. A knowledge-based repertoire might include the skills of describing, identifying, and providing examples and non-examples of a concept. A performance-based repertoire might include demonstrating skills in rehearsal and with a client across settings and stimuli (Sellers et al., 2016).

Developing knowledge- and performance-based repertoires in your supervisees involves a combination of activities, including instruction, rehearsal, and feedback. Instruction can be delivered in many ways, including by assigning readings and videos, discussing concepts verbally, and sometimes providing written material that you develop for specific purposes.

When you prepare such material as a supervisor, it is advisable to align the content with the standards of the credentialing body that the supervisee is being prepared for, or those of the organization employing the staff member under supervision. It may also be appropriate to create materials that allow for the development of professionalism and soft skills that are not specifically behavior analytic but important for any professional or paraprofessional in a human services industry. You should also consider your supervisee's history and cultural variables when creating written content for their supervision. Remember to use language that is inclusive and representative in ways that are meaningful for your supervisee.

Some of the written material that you may prepare for supervisees is likely to be similar to the clinical documentation that you use as a behavior analyst and that they may use in the future if they become credentialed. Even if your supervisees are not seeking credentialing, they likely need to read and understand clinical documentation. Therefore, it may be helpful to provide them with sample documents and case studies for evaluation and discussion. Samples may be actual clinical documents that have been de-identified or may be completely made up, with hypothetical information and data.

Sample documentation should include enough information to facilitate a good discussion of the principles you are teaching. Ideally, you will provide samples that offer a breadth of examples within the range of work that your supervisee is currently doing and will be doing in the future. For example, if your supervisee is working mostly with children and wants to work in a school setting, sample documents associated with treatment of adult clients would not be as helpful to their training.

Sample documents should also be of high quality to provide a good model. Use samples that illustrate the ideal of what documentation should look like and point out the relevant features to supervisees. Alternatively, you can use poorly written documentation as a teaching tool. In this situation, you can ask supervisees to review documentation and make corrections or highlight problem areas and explain why changes are needed. If you create samples for this purpose, be sure to clearly label them as having deliberate errors so that they are not misunderstood.

Other written materials that may be helpful in your supervision of supervisees and staff include flashcards or SAFMEDS, infographics, article summaries, and task analyses that outline different job requirements for behavior analysts. Supervisees may benefit from creating such materials themselves, so it may be helpful to work on these materials together or to assign your supervisee to create materials for you to review and provide feedback on. Use materials to facilitate discussion and learning, not as busy work.

Supervision Documentation

The materials discussed above are used to assist in skill acquisition and learning for those you are supervising. Outside of enhancing the knowledge and clinical skills of your supervisee, there are important documents related to supervision and feedback that are often used, including contracts and meeting notes.

Supervision Contracts

Planning is needed prior to the start of a supervision relationship. If you are supervising a candidate working towards a credential, the credentialing body may require that you formalize that relationship with the creation and signing of a supervision contract. If a contract is required, be sure to follow all guidelines for the contract that have been set by the credentialing organization. Even if a contract is not required, however, it may be helpful to create a contract with your supervisee.

A contract sets an occasion for a supervisor and a supervisee to discuss roles, responsibilities, and expectations (Kazemi et al., 2018). The language in the supervision contract should be clear, unambiguous, and informative. The supervision contract should be written and signed prior to the onset of the supervision relationship, and the supervisor and supervisee may choose to revisit and revise the contract as needed during the course of the supervision relationship. The contract should describe clear expectations and behaviors of the supervisor and supervisee (Sellers et al., 2016). Expectations might include submitting work one day before the supervision meeting, signing supervision notes, providing mutual feedback to each other, and updating any required documentation.

Example:

> Supervisor and supervisee agree to respect the time and space of clinical supervision by adhering to agreed appointments and allocated times. Both parties to this agreement will respect privacy, and all efforts will be made to reduce and eliminate interruptions of supervision sessions. Any party to this agreement who wishes to change meeting times, dates, or length of sessions shall notify the other party at least 24 hours prior to the meeting that is affected. Both parties will agree upon a replacement time.

Non-example:

> Both parties will do their best to make it to supervision sessions.

Meeting Documentation

Meetings with your supervisees should be documented as required by any relevant credentialing organization and the work setting where supervision is taking place. Suggested documentation for meetings includes an agenda that is set ahead of time, permanent products created by your supervisee, and notes about the meeting discussion.

A supervision meeting agenda can include items such as any assignments or readings that should be completed ahead of the supervision meeting, a plan for new content that will be introduced and how it will be addressed (e.g., verbal discussion, watching videos, role play), time for discussion of current clinical work and/or coursework (if relevant), and review of progress towards current supervision goals. Ideally, you can collaborate on the agenda with your supervisee initially, and then, over time, they may start to set the agenda and take more responsibility for their supervision experience. The agenda should be written in a way that is clear and structured. Once you find an agenda format that works well for you and your supervisee, create a template that you can use from meeting to meeting.

Your supervisee's permanent products may become part of your supervision documentation. If your supervisee creates a clinical document, article summary, or other materials under your supervision, it is a good idea to keep a dated copy of their work. This can help you to review their progress over time, track their response to your feedback, and document the work you have been doing together. While you are not the creator of these documents, you may take a role in the assignment and organization of them, so consider them part of your supervision documentation.

Finally, each supervision meeting and observation should be memorialized in a written note. This note should be formatted according to credentialing and organizational guidelines, but minimally will include both your name and your supervisee's name, the date and time of the meeting or observation, what was discussed, what activities were conducted, and any feedback provided to your supervisee. Some supervisors will leave space on the agenda to fill in these details so that the agenda becomes the meeting note.

Your supervisee should be given copies of their meeting notes and should have the opportunity to clarify what was written. Strive for notes that are complete and that identify areas of strength and opportunities for growth. Consider your supervisee's preferences in receiving written feedback as well. Ideally, notes should be brief but informative; complete, but not overwhelming.

Do:

- Align all documents with expectations of the credentialing organization or workplace.
- Include both knowledge- and performance-based materials.
- Provide samples and examples.
- Use inclusive language that is meaningful to your supervisee.
- Use a contract with objective language regarding expectations.
- Use clear, structured language regarding expectations and due dates.
- Provide your supervisee with copies of materials and documentation.

Don't:

- Use subjective language in your meeting notes.
- Provide open-ended deadlines for assigned tasks.

Evaluations and Feedback

Part of the supervisor's role is to evaluate the performance of their supervisees. Well-written evaluations have the power to increase appropriate professional behavior, improve staff performance, and influence positive outcomes for clients. Poorly written evaluations can have the opposite effect, either serving as a neutral consequence to behavior that will then remain unchanged or, worse yet, decreasing appropriate behavior. Poorly written evaluations can even jeopardize rapport between the supervisor and supervisee.

Evaluating Supervisee Progress

When evaluations are discussed in a meeting between parties, written documentation of staff performance is recommended and typically a requirement of the company, and it is currently a requirement of the Behavior Analyst Certification Board's Ethics Code for Behavior Analysts (Behavior Analyst Certification Board, 2020). Written documentation is vital for making data-based decisions, a key process for behavior analysts and supervisors in all aspects of their work. It is also crucial for mediating any future disputes that might arise. Evaluations should be written such that they serve as a valuable teaching tool for supervisees and staff members.

The goal of an evaluation is to offer useful feedback for the development of complex skills. Evaluations and feedback delivery may be formal or informal, and may occur annually, bi-annually, quarterly, with a change in position or responsibilities, or more frequently for new supervisees. Informal evaluations may be more frequent. Evaluation and feedback should be provided based on the performance and needs of the supervisee and, ideally, with respect to the supervisee's preferred feedback delivery method. The final outcome of feedback should help the supervisee acquire skills while establishing and maintaining rapport, trust, and collaboration in the supervision relationship.

A skilled supervisor is reflective and responsive to how their supervisee is receiving feedback and monitors the effects of feedback to make continued changes and improvements (LeBlanc et al., 2020). The learning histories of supervisees and staff members may influence how feedback is received and therefore should inform your approach to performance evaluations. It is critical to get to know your staff and establish rapport with your supervisee so that ongoing supervision interactions can be more effective. We should learn about our supervisees' histories, cultures, strengths, and preferences and use this information to guide our approach to delivering effective, meaningful feedback.

Consider that supervisee evaluations and feedback may be read by other supervisors or team members and demonstrate respect for your supervisee in your writing. One important way to do this is to base your evaluation and feedback on actual performance, rather than assumptions about behavior or intentions. Just as with other types of behavioral assessments, written evaluations of supervisee performance should include objective data. Ideally, performance data should be collected across multiple observations to increase accuracy (Johnson et al., 2015). When collecting performance data, be sure to accurately document the date, time, and context of the observation. You should also be mindful that notes may be read by the person being observed or others in the organization, so write them in such a way that you would not mind sharing them with others.

Depending on the requirements of the organization or purpose of the evaluation, these data may be collected and presented very formally, including graphs, descriptions of scheduled observations, and de-identified client data if relevant to the focus of the evaluation. If the evaluation is less formal, it may be appropriate to describe spontaneous observations. Using observation or data as a basis for your evaluation helps to maintain objectivity and provides your supervisee with clear information about their performance.

A written evaluation should also include feedback to shape continued improvement. As a behavior analyst, you know that individual learning histories may play a role in how feedback is received, and research shows inconsistent results on its effectiveness (Johnson et al., 2015; Mangiapanello & Hemmes, 2015). This, of course, reminds us of the critical need to get to know staff and individualize feedback whenever possible (Daniels & Daniels, 2014), just as you would for your own client. With that in mind, the following guidelines are general recommendations, and, while they can serve as a useful starting point, you should adjust them as needed as you get to know your supervisees and according to company procedures.

Written feedback should be balanced and meaningful. It is not helpful to your supervisee to provide empty praise that does not clearly identify what was done well. Instead, provide specific examples and descriptions of correct responding that should be maintained or increased in the future. Similarly, corrective feedback should be specific and objective and delivered in an encouraging, or at least neutral, manner. Calling attention to errors is a first step in bringing about awareness of performance issues. Depending on the format of the written evaluation, procedures for correcting behavioral deficits or errors may be included, with specific goals and objectives for improvement.

Example:

> Tamara,
> You demonstrated excellent work performance this past month. You exceeded 2 of your established performance goals by completing an average of 37 reviews per week and responding to calls within 2 hours. You were close to meeting your third performance goal of auditing timesheets at a rate of 6 per hour, achieving an average of 4 per hour. Let's schedule a time to discuss how you can adjust to ensure you're able to hit your goals this coming month.

Non-example:

> Tamara,
> You demonstrated excellent work this past month. Your commitment is outstanding. It's a pleasure to have you around the office. Thank you for your efforts!

Evaluating the Effectiveness of Supervision

Supervisors should evaluate the effectiveness of their supervision interventions (Sellers et al., 2016). This may be accomplished partially through competency evaluations of supervisees, which will ideally reflect improvements across areas targeted by the supervisor. If improvements are not noted, this is a good indicator that the supervision and feedback system may need revision.

Other sources of information to help you evaluate the effectiveness of the supervision that you are providing include client outcomes and progress, and social validity measures such as feedback from supervisees. Client outcomes can be considered secondary outcomes of supervision; if your supervisee is improving in service delivery, we should see improvement in client progress. These data may need to be interpreted cautiously, however, as there are many different variables that can impact client outcomes.

Social validity is a direct measure of your supervisee's experiences under your supervision. When measuring a supervisee's experiences, we usually want to know how acceptable supervision practices are to them, how much they feel they are being helped by supervision, and any feedback they may have to improve supervision. While the easiest way to get these answers is to directly ask supervisees to share their thoughts, this can put both of you in an uncomfortable position. Remember that you are in a position of authority over your supervisee and need to set the occasion for them to safely report their experiences with honesty. For this reason, it may be best to use a written system for receiving feedback from your supervisees.

If you have multiple supervisees, you can create an anonymous survey that asks questions about supervision experiences. This is a nice way to allow people to share their thoughts very freely. Even if you give your supervisee a form to fill out for feedback on supervision that is not anonymous, it may be easier and more comfortable for them to respond with time to think and choose their wording. You can then use their responses to facilitate a collaborative discussion. Here are some suggestions for questions that may be used to assess social validity in supervision:

- What is the most helpful topic (or discussion, activity, project) that we have completed in supervision? How was it helpful to you?
- What kinds of supervision activities have the best outcomes for your work (or knowledge, understanding, studying)? What kinds of activities would you like to do more of in the future?
- What have we done in supervision that has been less helpful to you? Are there any supervision activities that you would like to do less often?
- How can I improve your experience as a supervisee? What feedback do you have to help me be a better supervisor for you?

Remember that, when we ask for feedback, it is important to be ready to receive that feedback without responding defensively. This is another good reason to receive written feedback from your supervisees, so you have time to reflect and decide how to respond in a way that facilitates a collaborative relationship. Soliciting feedback from your supervisees on a regular basis can help to normalize the process and make it more comfortable and natural for everyone. While this type of feedback is not the same as getting feedback on assignments from an instructor, the suggestions for how to respond to corrective feedback remain consistent. If you are interested in reviewing our suggestions related to responding to corrective feedback, please find this in the "Assignments" section of Chapter 2 of this book.

Do:

- Evaluate the performance of both the supervisor and supervisee.
- Provide written documentation of all feedback.
- Deliver feedback according to the supervisee's style preference.
- Provide data to support the feedback you are giving.
- Use clear and objective language.
- Establish rapport with your supervisee prior to evaluating and providing feedback.
- Remember that written feedback is kept as a permanent product of progress.
- Provide both positive and corrective feedback, while ensuring that all feedback is genuine.
- Provide an opportunity for anonymous feedback, if possible.

Don't:

- Retain feedback documentation that is not shared with the person being evaluated.
- Provide evaluation documents to others without consent.
- Provide positive feedback that is vague or not genuine.

Self-Reflection Station

1   Reflect on your experience as a supervisee. Did you receive a structured and competency-based curriculum that guided your experience or was there less structure and guidance on what you learned? What lessons did you take away from your supervisory experience to maintain that you felt were helpful? What are some mistakes your supervisor made that you are now using as non-examples?

Writing as a Supervisor 81

2 Consider your current routine for providing feedback to those you supervise. How often do you provide formal, formative feedback? What is your process for evaluating how effective your supervision is and what feedback to provide? Do you ever give your supervisee opportunities to provide feedback on your performance as a supervisor?

Practice: How Would You Respond?

Compare your responses to our recommendations at the end of this book.

1 You have recently started supervision with a graduate student and have noted multiple areas for improvement, including professionalism, punctuality, and interpersonal communication. The graduate student is canceling meetings at the last minute, attending supervision meetings late, and does not speak much during sessions. You offer your observations, attempting to determine what the function of these behaviors is, and the supervisee comments that they do not feel that you are effective as a supervisor and that your feedback is not helpful. How would you respond to this situation and solicit additional feedback?
2 You are a behavior analyst in a school setting overseeing a team of paraprofessionals. Among them, Luisa has shown exceptional skills in implementing behavior intervention strategies for students with special needs. Your task involves providing formal feedback and documentation of Luisa's performance, following school protocols and ethical standards. Your evaluation report emphasizes Luisa's successful interventions, collaboration, and dedication, while also suggesting areas for potential growth and further training. This documentation recognizes her achievements and acts as a roadmap for her continuous development. Now, step into the role of the behavior analyst and craft the feedback report for Luisa, acknowledging her accomplishments, offering valuable guidance, and ensuring compliance with the necessary standards and ethical considerations.

References

Beaulieu, L., & Jimenez-Gomez, C. (2022). Cultural responsiveness in applied behavior analysis: Self-assessment. *Journal of Applied Behavior Analysis, 55*(2), 337–356. doi:10.1002/jaba.907.

Behavior Analyst Certification Board. (2020). *Ethics code for behavior analysts.* https://bacb.com/wp-content/ethics-code-for-behavior-analysts/

Daniels, A. C., & Daniels, J. E. (2014). *Performance management: Changing behavior that drives organizational effectiveness.* Performance Management.

Johnson, D. A., Rocheleau, J. M., & Tilka, R. E. (2015.) Considerations in feedback delivery: The role of accuracy and type of evaluation. *Journal of Organizational Behavior Management, 35*(3–4), 240–258. doi:10.1080/01608061.2015.1093055

Kazemi, E., Rice, B., & Adzhyan, P. (2018). *Fieldwork and supervision for behavior analysts: A handbook.* Springer.

LeBlanc, L. A., Taylor, B. A., & Marchese, N. V. (2020). The training experiences of behavior analysts: Compassionate care and therapeutic relationships with caregivers. *Behavior Analysis in Practice, 13*(2), 387–393. doi:10.1007/s40617-019-00368-z

Mangiapanello, K. A., & Hemmes, N. S. (2015). An analysis of feedback from a behavior analytic perspective. *The Behavior Analyst, 38*, 51–75. doi:10.1007/s40614-014-0026-x

Sellers, T. P., Valentino, A. L., & LeBlanc, L. A. (2016). Recommended practices for individual supervision of aspiring behavior analysts. *Behavior Analysis in Practice, 9*(4), 274–286. doi:10.1007/s40617-016-0110-7

Turner, L. B., Fischer, A. J., & Luiselli, J. K. (2016). Towards a competency-based, ethical, and socially valid approach to the supervision of applied behavior analytic trainees. *Behavior Analysis in Practice, 9*, 287–298. doi:10.1007/s40617-016-0121-4

6 Writing as a Faculty Member

Dana Reinecke

Behavior analytic college and university faculty have many responsibilities that involve writing. In addition to scholarly writing, which is required for many faculty positions (see Chapter 7, Writing as a Researcher), faculty need to communicate effectively in writing with their students and colleagues. With the increase in online delivery of higher education, these skills become even more crucial (Easton, 2003). While in traditional face-to-face education and synchronous remote learning environments faculty may have opportunities to provide verbal feedback and content to students in real time, fully online and asynchronous remote teaching make this more difficult. Regardless of format, however, if you are teaching in higher education you will need to be able to provide some written feedback to learners at least some of the time. Additionally, you must provide content, instructions, and syllabi to learners in written format.

Faculty-Produced Documents

Syllabus

One important type of document that many faculty need to write is the course syllabus (Hockensmith, 1988). A course syllabus is essentially a contract between you as the teacher and the learner; it should be clear, unambiguous, and informative. It is generally not acceptable to change the syllabus after the course starts, and so it is extremely important to have the syllabus in its finalized format before presenting it to students. If a change must be made, it should not have a negative impact on students and should be communicated clearly and in writing, as an amendment to the syllabus.

The syllabus should include course logistics (e.g., time, date, place of in-person or online meetings, number of credits), instructor contact information, learning objectives, grading and other policies, and a schedule of events. The syllabus should be as detailed as necessary, but not so long that students don't bother to read it. Some faculty like to create visually appealing syllabi, including graphics and text boxes, and some prefer to keep it very simple. The most important factor in designing your syllabus is that it needs to be used by your students, so use whatever tools you may have at your disposal to increase motivation to read the syllabus. One fun idea is to bury a couple of very small errors in the syllabus (such as typos, not incorrect due dates or procedural information) and offer extra credit to those students who find the errors by a certain date.

Example:

> Assignments are due in weeks 3, 5, and 7. See below for detailed instructions and expectations for each assignment. You may hand assignments in early, but they might not be graded until after the assignment due date. Assignments may not be resubmitted after grading. Late assignments will be accepted with a penalty of 10% of the total points per day, for up to 3 days after the assignment due date. After this time period, late submissions will not be accepted and the assignment will be scored zero.

Non-example:

> Students are expected to complete several assignments throughout the course. These assignments will be posted the week before they are due. Late assignments are discouraged.

Course Content

As an instructor, you may also need to prepare various types of written course content documents for students to use. These may include study guides, guided notes, content summaries, and visual materials (e.g., slides) to support lectures. The function of the document determines what should be included and how it should be formatted. This type of instructor-generated content is usually meant to supplement, not replace, course materials such as textbooks and assigned articles. You should not get caught up in re-creating any materials that are already available, but rather think about what can be prepared that will enhance students' use of, and ability to understand, the published material.

For study guides, highlight the important content that you want students to focus on (Conderman & Bresnahan, 2010). If you are going to expect them to know content that is not included in the study guide, it is fair to let them know that.

Example:

> This study guide is meant to focus your attention on certain sections of Chapter 2. You are still responsible for knowing the rest of Chapter 2, however, so be sure to read and reflect on the entire assigned reading for this week.

Non-example:

> Review all sections of the study guide to prepare for the test on Chapter 2.

Content summaries may be used to supplement assigned readings on topics that are typically confusing for learners. Sometimes faculty notice that many students struggle with the same content every semester, and so they choose to create some additional materials to address that content. The important thing here is to provide something different and additional, not just to restate what is in the existing material.

Example:

> It can be tricky to discriminate between respondent and operant conditioning. Here's a table showing several examples of each to help you identify the differences.

Non-example:

> Review the sections on respondent and operant conditioning in this week's readings.

Slides are often used to provide visual support for verbal lectures and may be presented in-person, remotely, or asynchronously (i.e., as part of a recording). Remember that the purpose of the slide is to add visual content to engage the listener, and to clarify concepts. Therefore, long sections of prose are usually not helpful and may be distracting. Graphics that are funny, interesting, or informative are appropriate for slides, as well as key words and phrases.

Assignment Instructions

You may also need to create written instructions for assignments, as well as rubrics or scoring guides. The most important thing to remember when writing instructions is that they should be crystal clear. Use short, simple sentences and, ideally, separate important concepts across bullet points. The scoring guide or rubric must match the description of the assignment and the instructions. Clearly identify where students have choices (e.g., topics, format) and where they do not (e.g., use of APA formatting, length of paper). The best way to determine if an assignment's instructions, scoring guide, or rubric is well written is to test it out, and so you may want to revise these after using them and finding where students are more and less successful.

Example:

> Compare and contrast two schedules of reinforcement in a two-page paper not inclusive of title page and reference list. Clearly define and provide an example for each schedule. Explain how the two schedules are similar and how they are different. Cite references to support your definitions and the similarities and differences. Use proper APA formatting, including title page and reference list.

Non-example:

> Write a short paper about schedules of reinforcement. Show that you know what two schedules of reinforcement are and how they compare.

Do:

- Provide consistent information across all documents.
- Develop course materials that enhance required readings and activities, highlight important concepts, and use visual supports as appropriate.
- Give explicit instructions in assignments about what is required to earn a perfect score.
- Provide clear scoring guides/criteria/rubrics for assignments.
- Identify where students do and do not have choices within assignments.

Don't:

- Change the syllabus or leave out relevant information.
- Make the syllabus so long that no one will read it.
- Re-create or restate existing material for course content.
- Overwhelm learners with additional content.
- Make slides overly wordy and not visually appealing.
- Write extensive assignment instructions, with irrelevant or distracting information, that may be hard for learners to follow.

Providing Feedback

Faculty usually need to provide learners with written feedback on their assignments. Feedback may be formative or summative and is usually qualitative in nature. Simply putting a grade on an assignment may not be very informative to the student, but giving them written feedback provides an extended learning opportunity. This is especially true for assignments that build up to longer projects, or for assignments in formats that will be replicated later in the same or other courses. For example, if a student is taught to write a functional behavior assessment

(FBA) in one course, feedback on that assignment may be very useful when they encounter an assignment in another course that requires them to use an FBA to develop a behavior intervention plan (BIP).

Feedback should be given relatively quickly. Like any consequence for behavior, it is going to be most effective when it occurs close in time to the behavior. Ideally, you should combine positive and corrective feedback. If feedback is only positive, learners may start to disregard it as not informative, and if it is only corrective, learners may find it aversive and start to avoid it. Like the syllabus, feedback is only effective if the student reads it. You should try to identify the type and format of feedback that are most likely to be accessed by the learner, to make the best use of your own time. It may also be important to explicitly tell learners, and remind them periodically, that they should attend to feedback given on their assignments. Sometimes learners have not received qualitative feedback in prior classes and will not even realize that there is more to look at and learn from than their overall grade.

Remember that feedback is intended to provide positive reinforcement to increase desirable responding and to provide correction to decrease problematic responding. If these effects on behavior are not observed, consider several possibilities and make adjustments as needed: Learners may not have seen/accessed feedback; learners may not have understood feedback; or learners may not be sufficiently motivated by feedback.

Example:

> This is a thoughtful and well-developed example of a motivating operation present in your daily life. You identified it as a motivating operation, but is this a UMO or a CMO? I would argue this is a CMO. If you agree, reflect on if it's a CMO-R, CMO-S, or CMO-T.

Non-example:

> Not enough details on this example.

Example:

> Your example is a good one for a reflex. You have described the dust as the unconditioned stimulus eliciting the unconditioned response of sneezing. However, the discussion prompt is asking for a respondent conditioning example. What are the variables involved in respondent conditioning? What will the neutral stimulus be? How will this neutral stimulus acquire the eliciting properties to elicit a conditioned response? See if you can add more details to your scenario.

Non-example:

> Your scenario exemplifies a reflex and does not describe respondent conditioning.

Do:

- Provide feedback in a timely manner.
- Provide both positive and corrective feedback.
- Assess the impact of feedback and adjust as needed.
- Assess the type and format of feedback that are most likely to be useful to learners.

Don't:

- Overwhelm learners with vague positive feedback or extensive corrective feedback.
- Delay feedback so that learners are unable to benefit from it for future work.

Self-Reflection Station

1 Reflect on an experience in which you have been asked to develop a course or training. What were the most challenging components? What came naturally or easy? Create a list of five recommendations you would give to yourself, if you could go back in time, about how to be more efficient and interactive in your development.

2 Reflect on the feedback you received from instructors who have taught your courses in your academic training as a behavior analyst. What types of feedback did you receive, and how did it shape your behavior? Based on your experience, how would you provide feedback to a learner on their writing and case conceptualization?

Practice: How Would You Respond?

1 You have just been asked to design an introduction to a behavior analysis class for an undergraduate program. You want to ensure that the course is rigorous but not so overly complicated that it is beyond the scope of an assistant behavior analyst. Devise a short syllabus for a 12-week course. What topics would you cover? What book(s) would you include? What types of readings might you want to include?
2 You are developing a special topics seminar course in an area that you are incredibly passionate about. Create three assignments with instructions and rubrics for each to evaluate the learners consistently.

References

Conderman, G., & Bresnahan, V. (2010). Study guides to the rescue. *Intervention in School and Clinic*, *45*(3), 169–176. doi:10.1177/1053451209349532

Easton, S. S. (2003). Clarifying the instructor's role in online distance learning. *Communication Education*, *52*(2), 87–105. doi:10.1080/03634520302470

Hockensmith, S. F. (1988). The syllabus as a teaching tool. *The Educational Forum*, *52*(4), 339–351. doi:10.1080/00131728809335503

7 Writing as a Researcher

Julianne Lasley, Kaori Nepo, and Dana Reinecke

Research is an important area of knowledge for behavior analysts (Normand & Donohue, 2023; Sidman, 2011). As prospective behavior analysts, students and trainees learn about how to read and conduct experimental research (Weiss, 2018). Some graduate programs require students to design and implement research projects, and some professional behavior analysts work exclusively or partially in conducting research (Carr & Briggs, 2010; Shawler et al., 2018). The development and dissemination of research are writing-focused activities, and your writing skills as a researcher can have a big impact on how your research is received by others (Luiselli, 2010).

Your involvement with research may change over the course of your career. Some written products that you may create include literature reviews, research proposals, grant proposals, and manuscripts to be submitted for your degree (e.g., a thesis or dissertation) or for publication in a peer-reviewed journal. There are well-established conventions for each of these types of documents, in addition to organization- or school-specific guidelines. Some general considerations for research-related writing are shared in this chapter.

Literature Reviews

Writing a literature review in behavior analysis is similar to the process you would use for any field of psychology. Start by identifying your research topic (Briggs & Mitteer, 2022) and search criteria, locate related research, and organize and synthesize what you have learned into a coherent conclusion. Remember that a literature

DOI: 10.4324/9781003463498-7

review should not just be a series of summaries about different articles, but rather information compiled in a way that proves a point or leads to new questions and further research directions.

In behavior analysis there may be a few different reasons you are conducting a literature review, so, first, identify the purpose of your literature review (King et al., 2020). Are you justifying a proposal of research in the field, conducting a thesis or dissertation, or reviewing the literature to identify evidence-based treatments for a particular behavior of interest? Depending on the purpose, your audience may be more or less familiar with behavioral terminology. Regardless of the audience or purpose, a literature review is a piece of scholarly writing, and so it should be written in a way that is clear, concise, and well organized. Before you even start to write, however, there are several steps that need to be completed, as described below.

Identify the Research Topic

Identify the topic, intervention, or behavior of interest. The topic may be something very general or very specific, depending on the purpose of the literature review. If you are using your review of the literature to propose a certain intervention or as the introduction to a paper that you are going to submit for publication, you will probably have a very specific and focused topic. If you are writing a review to justify a line of research or a large project such as a thesis or dissertation, the topic may begin more broadly and become more specific throughout the literature review.

To determine the number of articles needed, you should reflect on why you are conducting your literature review. If you are conducting this review to write a behavior support plan, then it may be that a few very recent articles related to treatment of the behavior of interest are all you need. If you are writing a literature review for an assignment or research proposal, it will probably include a more thorough review of research to date on the topic of interest, including seminal articles that represent the very first writing on the topic. The most thorough literature reviews would be those that are being used for a dissertation, thesis, or a systematic review (King et al., 2020) of the literature for publication in an article.

Identify Search Criteria

You will likely use one or more digital databases to search for articles to include in your literature review. Choose a database that will be most likely to yield results related to your topic. Some databases that may be preferred when searching topics within the behavior analysis domain include PsycInfo, ERIC, EBSCO, ProQuest, PsycArticles, PsycBooks, PubMed, and PsycExtra. Google Scholar is also a free and readily available starting point for locating studies.

Search terms are entered into the database individually and in combination with each other to generate lists of publications. It is important to be thoughtful about the search terms you use, so that you are not overwhelmed with too many results or do not find enough articles. For example, if you search "ABA and autism," you will probably find many thousands of results – far too many to sift through. If you search "ABA and autism and PECS," however, you will likely find a more manageable list to review. If your search yields few relevant articles, it may be helpful to use the thesaurus most likely located in your chosen database to find other suggested search terms.

Example:

> Search terms for research related to the treatment of vocal manding: manding, vocalizations, requesting items, applied verbal behavior, language acquisition.

Non-example:

> Search terms for research related to the treatment of vocal manding: vocal manding.

Each database is different, but most include options for refining searches in various ways. For example, you might be able to filter results by date of publication. This would be helpful if you are seeking only the most recent articles about a specific intervention for the purposes of supporting a behavior intervention plan. If, however, you are conducting a literature review to support your thesis proposal, you should probably look for articles going back as far as possible to capture the development of this line of research and show how it leads to current research questions.

Another filter that allows you to exclude books, newspapers, dissertations, and other non-peer-reviewed sources may be available. When writing a literature review, it is best to focus on peer-reviewed journal articles from reputable journals. A book or dissertation is likely to present a literature review, which is not something that you would use in your own literature review. Your review should be of primary sources, not another author's interpretation of those sources. You can also choose to include journal titles in your searches, which can help to focus your research on behavior-analytic journals. Some suggested journals are: *Journal of Applied Behavior Analysis, Journal of the Experimental Analysis of Behavior, Behavior Analysis in Practice, Psychological Record, The Analysis of Verbal Behavior, Journal of Organizational Behavior Management, Behavioral Interventions, Journal of Autism and Developmental Disorders, Perspectives on Behavior Science, Behavior and Social Issues*, and *Journal of Contextual Behavioral Science.*

Identify Articles for Review

Deciding which articles you will include in your review can be fun and also time-consuming. If you read every article in full, you may spend a lot of time reading, which can be inspiring and engaging, but won't help get your literature review written. As you are finding articles, you can most efficiently sift through them by first reading titles and abstracts. After reading the abstract, you should have a decent idea of whether this topic is related. Read through the entire article after vetting the abstract.

Once you have found some useful articles, you can expand your reference list by mining for more resources from the reference lists of the articles you have already. This is a great way to find seminal, original works on the topic that you are interested in. You may not wish to mine the reference list from every article, but using this technique with one or two articles that are important to your review can be very helpful.

Another way to find more articles is to use a search tool such as Google Scholar to find works that have cited a particular article. First, search for an article that you have already read and found useful. Then, click on "cited by" for a list of articles, books, and other resources that have cited this article. This is a nice way to trace the progress of a line of research and works well with articles that may be from several years ago but are very relevant to the topic you are examining. Some academic databases may also include a way to search for works where a resource has been cited, so it is worth asking a reference librarian how to do this if it is not readily apparent.

Organize the Articles

Now that you have several articles, the next step is to organize them in a way that supports your efficient use of the information to build your literature review (Cone & Foster, 1993). It's a good idea to develop a consistent system so that you can refer back to previously reviewed research in future projects. There are some great options for organizing articles, including commercially available apps and software. You can also start your own organization system by creating a spreadsheet or table.

Think about how you want to sort these articles. Some examples of ways to sort or organize articles include chronologically, by topic, by effectiveness of intervention, by behavior, and by intervention. Next, create columns to collect all of the information you want on each of the articles. These columns might include: Article title, keywords, link to article, fully formatted reference, brief summary of the main point of the article, strengths/limitations, and a final column for extra notes. Then you can list each article in a separate row, filling in the information for each of the columns. See Table 7.1 for an example.

It also may be helpful to keep an annotated bibliography as you are reviewing articles. This strategy allows you to note the most important points about each article by briefly summarizing the article in a few short sentences or bullet points. Another strategy is to write a one-sentence summary of each article, so that you have a record in your own words of what is important about the articles you are including in your review.

Table 7.1 Sample table for organizing articles.

Article Title	Key Words	Reference	Summary	Other Notes
Some current dimensions of applied behavior analysis	applied, behavioral, analytic, generality, conceptual systems, effective, technological	Baer, D. M., Wolf, M. M., & Risley, T. R. (1968). Some current dimensions of applied behavior analysis. *Journal of Applied Behavior Analysis, 1(1)*, 91–97. https://doi.org/10.1901/jaba.1968.1-91	Seminal article defining how ABA practice is defined	Check out follow-up articles expanding on these dimensions

Evaluate the Studies

Next, you'll need to evaluate each of the articles that you have gathered and make some decisions about if they fit into your review and, if so, what meaningful contribution they will make to the point of your review. Read each study carefully and critically. It may be helpful to guide your review with a set of questions, such as the following:

- How does this article relate to the topic of interest?
- How effective was the intervention? Did it work? Were the effects of the intervention worth the effort involved?
- Was experimental control shown in the research design? How confident could a reader be that the intervention caused the change in behavior?
- Were there any other variables that may be responsible for the behavior change? Was the study set up to rule out any extraneous variables so you believe that the manipulated variable was the one responsible for the change?
- Was this research socially valid and relevant to your topic of interest?

Synthesize Information: Putting It All Together

A good literature review is more than a summary of articles and is rather a synthesis that takes existing knowledge and explains it in such a way that the reader is led to a conclusion or question that they didn't have when they started reading. Think of a literature review as a road map that takes your reader from their current state of knowledge about a topic, through what they may not know, to what you want them to understand about what all that information together means. How you synthesize your review depends on the purpose of your literature review.

If you are writing a literature review to support a research proposal, you may want to start with an introduction to the problem that the research study is designed to solve, followed by some theoretical background information. Then, you can dive into a synthesis of related articles, demonstrating what you learned from each article and how these articles work together. Every study that you review should provide information to support your research question. Such information can include validation of the existence of the problem, but, for most research proposals, you want to show what has been done to try to solve this problem and what your research will do to further those investigations. A literature review for a research proposal should show why your research question is important and why your plans for addressing that question are correct. Organization is crucial in this kind of literature review, because you are building a case or an argument. Be very mindful of the order of information that you present, aiming for a logical progression from problem to solution.

If you are writing a literature review to support a clinical intervention, then your research review is probably brief and very much to the point. Unlike the literature review needed for a research proposal, in this case, you simply want to point to the existence of research to support your intervention as an evidence-based practice. You do not need to synthesize or build an argument. Your review may include brief summaries of a few recent, relevant articles with a focus on the actual intervention, data collection procedures, and effectiveness of treatment. Sometimes, your literature review may include just a citation of the article supporting the effectiveness of the intervention, with a reference to that intervention on a references page.

The literature review in a dissertation or thesis is very thorough. These types of reviews may start with an introduction to the topic and the rationale for study and then offer a very thorough discussion of the theoretical background behind the area of study. Next, you will tell a story about all of the research related to this topic that leads to the current research questions. Depending on the expectations of the university where the dissertation or thesis manuscript is being written, you may be expected to find and discuss all of the prior research in a given area or only seminal and recent articles.

Do:

- Consider your audience and purpose of the review.
- Consider how to best organize your readings and take notes on your findings.
- Create an outline.
- Set small goals and work on it over time.
- Use a notecard or visual prompt to remind you of what information you are seeking as you sift through articles.

Don't:

- Procrastinate and attempt to throw the review together quickly without planning.
- Go down unnecessary rabbit holes.
- Assume you will remember details from the articles after you have read them once, without any notes.

Research Proposals

Writing a sound, compelling research proposal is a necessary first step in any research endeavor (Cone & Foster, 1993). Consider the proposal to be both a request for permission to conduct your research and a guidebook for how your study will be conducted. As such, a research proposal needs to be clear, detailed, well written, and thorough, while also not being overly complicated or including extraneous information. A research proposal may be required for requesting and obtaining permission to recruit participants and conduct research at a certain site, such as a school or agency. It is also required as part of an institutional review board (IRB) application, which it is necessary to submit for ethical oversight. You may also use a research proposal to obtain approval for thesis or dissertation work, or as part of a grant submission. As always, the specific requirements for a research proposal will depend on where you are submitting it and for what purpose, but there are some general guidelines that can be helpful for any research proposal.

Justification for Research

Bear in mind that a research proposal is ultimately a request for permission. You should approach it as an opportunity to lay out a justification for the research that you would like to conduct, with enough information for the reader to conclude that this research is a good idea. A justification for research usually includes a literature review that shows that your proposed project is necessary to further understanding in a given area (see the section on writing a literature review earlier in this chapter). Be mindful of your audience and provide sufficient detail about the background of the research problem and prior solutions for your readers to follow the argument you are making. For example, if you are proposing a study about natural environment teaching (NET) to an IRB that does not see many behavior analytic projects, you need to start by explaining behavior analytic interventions as a context before going into the relevant studies on NET that lead to your proposal. At the same time, do not overwhelm your readers with too much information. Be sure that all the background information points to your proposal, and that there is no extraneous information. You don't want your reader to lose focus or interest in your proposal.

Research Plan

A research proposal also includes a detailed plan or protocol for how the research will be conducted. Write this section as though you are providing details to someone else to actually carry out the research protocol. Include details about the type of participants you will be seeking, how you will recruit them, and what the consent procedures will consist of. Identify any setting or materials requirements for the research. Explain how data will be collected, stored, and analyzed. Describe the research design and exactly what will happen in each condition of the study, in detail. Remember to include plans for collecting interobserver agreement and treatment fidelity data.

Being as thorough as possible in this section serves two important purposes. First, you can demonstrate to the reader of your proposal that you are thoughtful and prepared in your approach. You know what the research will entail and you have planned for all possibilities. Second, you will ensure that, if your project is approved, there will be no surprises, and you will have good documentation of what has been agreed.

Projected Outcomes

If you are proposing applied research that is aimed to demonstrate the effectiveness of an intervention, it may be helpful to include a description of expected results (Cone & Foster, 1993). You may even include a graph of hypothetical data, but, if you do this, it should be clearly labeled as such so that it is not misunderstood to be actual pilot data. Your projected outcomes should be reasonable and realistic, and you should provide some rationale from the literature or based on the applicable theories to explain why you anticipate these results.

Known Limitations and Delimitations

It is a good idea to brainstorm areas of your proposed research that may be seen as limitations and explain these in the proposal. Applied research will nearly always have some areas of weakness, and so understanding and discussing them in advance is helpful to show that you fully understand the implications of your proposal. Limitations may occur in measurement, design, and ability to implement procedures with fidelity. There may also be limitations associated with data loss if participants are unable or unwilling to engage in all research activities. Limitations are often the result of the researcher's efforts to protect the participants and to engage in ethical research, and so explaining these reasons for known limitations can help your reader to understand why you are making certain choices. Other perceived limitations may actually be delimitations, or variables that you have chosen not to study at this time, which is worth explaining to the reader of your proposal.

Remember That the Review Process Is Iterative

Submitting a research proposal to an ethics review board or other authority is intimidating. A collection of individuals, who may not fully understand your science, will be picking apart your study and requiring changes that may seem integral to your study. It is important to remember that the process of creating a proposal is an interactive and iterative process that will require you to make adjustments and compromises. Your study is not just yours, but that of every individual who will have a hand in the development and approval of it throughout the process. Be flexible with your ideas and embrace the review process as an opportunity for professional growth.

Do:

- Be mindful of your audience.
- Provide a clear justification for your research.
- Provide a detailed research plan.
- Project realistic outcomes.

Don't:

- Overwhelm your reader with too much information.
- Avoid identifying limitations and delimitations.

Grant Proposals

Grant writing may sound overwhelming, especially when you tackle this task for the first time. Writing for a grant is not something that every behavior analyst does, but, if this is something that interests you, there are numerous grants available for research projects, business opportunities, and professional development. Grant opportunities may be very specific, providing funding only for certain types of projects, while others may be much more open to a range of different proposals. Grants can also be very large, paying out huge budgets over years, or very small, providing only limited funding to offset research or travel expenses. No matter what type of grant you are writing for, there are several suggested steps for working toward a successful grant proposal.

Search for Grants

First, you need to understand and identify what grants are available and relevant to your project. A good way to search for grants is to use keywords in the search bar on a grants website, such as grants.gov. For example, if you are interested in seeking funds for a research project to enhance technology for training practitioners who work with individuals who have intellectual and developmental disabilities, you may want to use keywords such as "technology," "training," and "IDD." Grants websites will provide you with lists of available grants, awarded projects, application forms, and necessary information for the application forms. In addition to government-funded grants, you can look into research organizations, behavior analysis associations, nonprofits, and your own employer to see if grants are offered.

Evaluate Resources

Once you identify the grants that are relevant to your project, you should check on available resources in your team or organization. If such resources are available, you also need to consider the time and effort needed to write the grant proposal relative to the potential positive outcomes. The obvious benefit of winning a grant is funding, but also remember that obtaining a grant may be valuable for your curriculum vitae (CV) and look appealing to current and future employers, even if the award is not for a lot of money. Here are some questions that can help you to evaluate resource availability and if resources should be allocated to writing a grant:

- Do you have support from the organization or your team to complete the project?
- Do you have the time to gather information and write the application without compromising your work?

- Grants often require the organization or project team to match the funds. If the grant requires matching funds, are those funds available?
- Are you able to proceed with your project if you do not receive the grant?
- Would writing a grant proposal and/or winning a grant help support a future job application or promotion in your current employment?

Read and Understand

Take the time to fully read the grant announcement, or functional opportunity announcement (FOA), at least a few times. It is important to understand the award criteria and make sure your project fits these criteria. Pay attention to which materials and documentation are required for the proposal. Enlisting two or three colleagues to also read the announcement can be helpful to avoid misunderstanding of these criteria and overall eligibility for the grant. Check and understand the due dates of the application also, since it is common to have a series of due dates for a grant application. You may find that you are not required to submit the full application for the first review. You should create a checklist and plan your process to complete each document in order to meet the requirements and deadlines.

Write Your Proposal

Finally, you can start to craft your application! Many grant websites require you to register to access application forms and other information. You may need to register to multiple systems. It is helpful to spend time reviewing tutorials and exploring the site to get familiar with the portal. You'll have to identify what forms you need and where to upload these forms by each deadline.

When you are crafting the proposal, your goals and objectives should be clearly and operationally defined while meeting the requirements or criteria of the specific grant. Choose language so your need statements fit the purview of the grant without changing your project. If you find that you are changing your project to fit the grant, this grant might not be the most appropriate for your project, and you may need to research other available grants. Remember that your audience may not be familiar with ABA terminology or jargon, so be sure to define terms as you need to use them and avoid overly complicated explanations.

You need to include citations and statistics (i.e., a literature review) to justify your project. Your statements should be based on the facts and demonstrate the gaps in research and how your project would contribute to the local community, society, or scientific community. See the section on writing a literature review earlier in this chapter for tips on building a good synthesis of the literature that supports a research proposal.

Finally, your grant proposal needs to include support for your capacity and resources to carry out the project efficiently and effectively. It is helpful to describe your experience with similar projects. For example, your research experience and publications would be critical to describe in support of your capacity for the research grants. You also need to describe the available resources necessary for the project, to show that, if you do obtain the grant funds, you will be able to fulfill the project.

Do:

- Create a checklist for yourself including the criteria for eligibility, the required information/documents, and all relevant due dates.
- Register for the grant using a professional email address and become familiar with the portal.
- Operationally define all goals.
- Use technical and conceptually systematic language to describe the impact and needs of your study.
- Provide your personal experience and demonstrate your ability to match funds as necessary.
- Include a thorough literature review that provides a solid basis for your study's merit and ability to fill gaps in the current literature.
- Create a budget that is reasonable but still demonstrates the necessity of the funding.

Don't:

- Assume that your name will speak for itself.
- Procrastinate on completing the grant proposal.
- Submit generalized or colloquial descriptions of the study.
- Skim through research announcements.
- Be too narrow in your research ideas when searching for grants.

Disseminating Scholarly Work

Contributing to the knowledge base of the field can be a very rewarding activity for behavior analysts. Contributions may be made in several ways, including conference presentations (workshops, symposia, or posters), webinars, and publication of journal articles and books. Such activities are available to anyone with the time for, and interest in, contributing and are encouraged for graduate students and clinicians who wish to share their work and develop their professional résumés (or CVs). Following are descriptions of various ways to share your scholarly work. There are some general tips and strategies to keep in mind for each of these opportunities, but you should always check the submission guidelines for the specific conference, journal, or publisher you are interested in working with and be sure to follow those closely.

Conference Presentations

You probably already know that attending a conference is a great way to find out about the latest research, earn continuing education units (CEUs), and network with other professionals (Becerra et al., 2020). Presenting at a conference also allows others to get to know you and your work and is a wonderful opportunity to strengthen your professionalism and practice scholarly communication skills. In addition to the bigger national and international conferences, many state and regional associations also have smaller conferences, so you can choose the venue that best suits your work and comfort level with presenting.

Most of the time, ideas for conference presentations are proposed using a formal process and then peer-reviewed to determine if the proposed event is accepted. You will find out how to submit for a conference when a call for papers is published, so keep an eye on the websites or social media channels associated with the conferences you are interested in presenting at. The call for papers provides information about what types of presentations are sought, what information is needed for a complete proposal that can be reviewed, and the timeline for submissions and decisions.

After carefully reading the call for papers, you should work together with any co-presenters to develop a proposal that is complete and meets criteria. A call for papers often asks for presenter information, such as a CV and/or bio; the audience size and level for whom the presentation is designed; what materials or handouts you plan to provide; and details about the proposed presentation, including title, abstract, and learning objectives.

When preparing your proposal, think about the audience that you are hoping to reach so that you can match the level of content to the experience level of the audience. The title should convey enough information for the audience to have a reasonable expectation of the contents and level of the presentation. Depending on the venue, you may want to create a catchy title that will appeal to audience members who may be choosing between several different, simultaneous events. The abstract is a brief paragraph summarizing your proposed presentation, including the methods and results if you are presenting about research. Learning objectives are statements of what the audience should expect to know or be able to do after attending the session. It is usual to identify three or four learning objectives for every hour of a presentation.

Remember to proofread your submission and be sure to keep a copy of what you have submitted. Some electronic submission portals do not allow you to return to your submission later on. If your proposal is accepted, you will need to create a presentation that matches the information provided.

Poster Presentations

Poster presentations are a great way for students or early career professionals to get started in presenting. A poster is a visual presentation of work, usually presented during an event where conference attendees can walk around and review posters. As a poster presenter, you would be available to discuss your work and answer questions, and so it is not necessary to include all the information on your poster.

An effective and visually appealing poster typically includes bullet points for the most important information, along with graphs, tables, or other illustrations that help to convey the main points or results (Beins & Beins, 2020). For a poster presenting the results of a single-subject design research project, you may have a few bullet points outlining the relevant literature and rationale for the research, a brief description of the methods, and a figure showing the results.

A poster is created within a slide presentation program as one single slide that is then printed on a large sheet of paper. The conference organizers will notify you about what size your poster should be. It is usually acceptable to be creative with colors, graphics, and fonts on a poster. Sometimes, academic programs and organizations have templates that are preferred for poster presentations. When styling your poster, be mindful that you want your audience to be able to read the poster from a few feet away, so aim for a clear, large font and an uncluttered presentation.

Slide Presentations

Conference presentations other than posters are often delivered orally and accompanied by visual supports such as slide presentations and videos. Two examples of such presentations, workshops and symposia, are described below. For both types of events, visual supports should be used to enhance, rather than distract from, the presentation.

Slide presentations can be fun to make and give you an opportunity to get creative. Some software programs include templates and suggestions for making your slides visually appealing. Be careful not to overdo animations or transitions, and make sure that any images used are relevant and have a clear purpose.

Text should be used sparingly on slide presentations. Avoid writing large blocks of text, which may distract your audience as they try to read while you speak. It is also easy to fall into the habit of reading your slides instead of talking naturally, which can be a less engaging presenting style. You may want to add additional notes to yourself in the Notes section of your slides, which can be printed for you to reference during your presentation or show only to you when using Presenter View.

Your presentation can be made more interactive by embedding audience participation opportunities into your slides. These can be shared using polling or other interactive apps that audience members can access from their phones. If you do use an interactive app, be sure to test your connectivity and audience access to the activity when you are in the conference venue. You can also use a lower-tech approach and include questions or images on your slides that prompt audience responses at times when you pause and invite people to share their thoughts.

Workshops

Experienced behavior analysts may present workshops, which are verbally presented and include interactive components. A workshop is typically a longer event, lasting for 2 hours or more. Workshops are training events that teach attendees a particular skill and often include access to materials that attendees can take with them for future use.

Written materials that may be generated to support workshops include slide presentations, handouts, and activities such as guided notes, worksheets, checklists, instruments, and other tools. When preparing written materials for workshops, be sure that the materials are aligned with the content of the workshop. During the workshop, interactive audience activities may require written materials such as case studies or worksheets. Design these materials with your audience level and size in mind. Will you have attendees work independently or in small groups? Will you ask attendees to consider cases from their own experience, or provide them with sample data and case descriptions?

Consider what content would be helpful for your attendees to refer to later, such as reference lists, treatment integrity checklists, data sheets, and any other practical tools. Workshops are designed to provide actionable training, and people who invest time and money in attending workshops expect to leave with skills that they can implement independently. Workshop presenters may have printed materials available for attendees to take with them or may instead choose to store materials in a cloud-based environment and provide a link or QR code for attendees to access the materials. If you choose to share materials via the cloud, consider putting a time limit on access and notify attendees what that time limit is. Also, be sure that the sharing link allows for downloading but not editing of the documents, or someone may inadvertently delete or change the documents during the access period. Finally, it is reasonable to identify documents as associated with your name or company by adding a watermark or logo.

Symposia

A symposium is a way to deliver one or more short-form presentations. The format of a symposium is established by the conference organizers and may vary by length and number of individual presentations, as well as by whether or not a chair or discussant is included. A symposium usually aims to deliver similar content around a theme, but the theme may be very broad or very specific. Some conference organizers will also group short presentations together in symposia even if they do not have a common theme, for scheduling purposes.

When preparing a symposium presentation, focus on providing succinct but thorough information. You may only have 15 or 20 minutes to speak, depending on the conference guidelines. Practice giving your talk several times to ensure that you are within the right time frame. Consider including some opportunities for audience interaction or to take questions, but be sure to account for these in your overall time so that you don't go over your time.

Written materials associated with symposia include slide presentations and, sometimes, handouts. Some speakers provide a printed copy or link to a cloud-stored handout, often consisting of the slide presentation saved as a PDF with several slides on a page. Another format for handouts is a one-page summary of important information, such as definitions of terms, links to helpful information, a reference list, or descriptions of procedures.

Webinars

Webinars have become popular as technology has improved and become more accessible, and current events have demanded options for remote meetings. Webinars can be conducted by almost anyone with a computer and some technical skill, using free or paid software and reaching small or large audiences. Whether you are invited to present a webinar or choose to offer one on your own or with a few colleagues, there are some good practices to follow.

First, remember that your audience members are participating from their own environment. That means they will have distractions that will be easier to attend to than if they were in a physical space with you and other attendees. If you are concerned with keeping your audience's attention, provide opportunities for active responding and interaction. There are many different audience participation apps available and doubtless more emerging regularly, but it can be as easy as inviting people to answer questions in chat. In smaller groups, you can also invite attendees to unmute for participation.

The slide presentation is likely the most important and possibly the only written material associated with a webinar. Following the guidance provided above will help you to develop a visually engaging backdrop for your webinar that adds supportive content without being too distracting. If you are going to provide a digital handout, consider consolidating important content and adding links to other resources in a PDF and making that available by uploading to the chat or sharing on the cloud or a website.

Journal Articles

Publication in a scholarly journal is a great achievement. Although publishing your work in a peer-reviewed journal requires a high level of scholarly writing and critical thinking, there are no limitations on who can submit to a journal for publication. Some articles that are published in well-known behavior analytic journals are authored by undergraduate, graduate, and doctoral students. Many are based on doctoral or master's research and consist of a brief summary of dissertation or thesis research. Some are written by clinical practitioners who are not associated with a university program. In the field of behavior analysis, you do not have to be on university faculty to conduct and share your research.

When preparing a manuscript for publication, you may have a good idea of which journal you want to submit to, but you do not need to know for sure when you get started. It is important to decide what kind of article you want to write, however. There are many options in the behavior analytic literature, including literature reviews, commentaries, meta-analyses, and experimental research papers. Articles may also be of varying lengths, from brief reports to multi-experiment studies. Read several examples of the type of paper you are writing to see what kind of information is usually included and how the authors present the information. As you write your paper, you will be reading and referring to the literature that supports the main points you are making or the research you have conducted, so be mindful of these papers as models that you can emulate.

While writing, keep track of the sources you are citing and maintain your reference list. There are some resource tracking and citing programs that can help you to do this, or you can simply add sources to your reference list as you use them. When the paper is complete, look at the reference list, see which journals were cited from most frequently, and consider submitting your work to one of these.

Just like when pursuing a grant or submitting for a conference presentation, when preparing a manuscript to submit for publication, carefully review the submission guidelines of the journal you are planning to submit to. Publishers have their own requirements for how documents are submitted (Luiselli, 2010). For example, many publishers require the title page to not have any author names or affiliations, so that the reviewers can read the paper blindly, or without knowing who wrote it.

Many scholarly articles are written by groups of authors, and so you may be working with other writers on a paper. It is very advisable to establish roles and authorship order early on in this situation so that everyone understands what work they are agreeing to contribute and how their contributions will be acknowledged. The order of authors is determined by the level of contribution and work done by each party.

After working with your co-authors on writing, proofreading, and formatting your submission, there is a big sigh of relief when you finally submit! Be prepared to wait for a response, however. Journals may take several months to review and make a decision about your manuscript. If your paper is accepted, congratulations! If not, the journal editor may ask you to make revisions and resubmit, or may decline to publish your paper. While this may be disappointing, you will also, probably, receive good feedback from the reviewers that you can use to refine your work and submit it to another journal. No matter what, the process of writing and submitting your scholarly work is an engaging and rewarding professional activity, which could lead to the reward of seeing your work in print and sharing it with others in the field.

Do:

- Always check specific submission guidelines.
- Review the submission timeline related to original submission and decision.
- Proofread all written material.
- Practice presenting written material out loud if you are submitting for an oral presentation.
- Use visual supports to enhance your presentation.
- Embed audience participation when applicable.
- Identify handouts with watermark or logo.

Don't:

- Procrastinate when preparing yourself and your materials.
- Go over your allotted time.
- Assume acceptance for every submission.
- Get discouraged if you are denied; use it as a learning opportunity and try again.

Self-Reflection Station

1 Reflect on an experience with attempting to publish your research. What was your experience regarding the writing experience? Did you find it a difficult process or were you able to just "knock it out"? How do you maintain motivation to complete academic/scholarly writing?
2 Consider your current attitudes toward the peer-review process. Do you enjoy the process of writing these types of projects or do you usually avoid them? Is doing this type of research in alignment with your values?

Practice: How Would You Respond?

1 You are attempting to write a research proposal for an IRB at a university and you are having a difficult time writing in a way that would be approachable to a non-behavior analytic reviewer. Using the information you learned in this chapter as well as the information in Chapter 4 regarding working with non-behavior analytic colleagues, craft two paragraphs that would explain the scientific merit of your study while maintaining language that would be appropriate for a diverse audience.

2 Consider a research study that you would like to conduct. Search for a grant proposal that is currently active and begin the process. Create a rough draft of your proposal and send it to a colleague to review and validate. Be open to feedback and remember that academic writing is a process!

References

Becerra, L. A., Sellers, T. P., & Contreras, B. P. (2020). Maximizing the conference experience: Tips to effectively navigate academic conferences early in professional careers. *Behavior Analysis in Practice, 13* (2), 479–491. doi:10.1007/s40617-019-00406-w

Beins, B. C., & Beins, A. M. (2020). *Effective writing in psychology: Papers, posters, and presentations.* John Wiley.

Briggs, A. M., & Mitteer, D. R. (2022). Updated strategies for making regular contact with the scholarly literature. *Behavior Analysis in Practice, 15*(2), 541–552. doi:10.1007/s40617-021-00590-8

Carr, J. E., & Briggs, A. M. (2010). Strategies for making regular contact with the scholarly literature. *Behavior Analysis in Practice, 3*(2), 13–18. doi:10.1007/BF03391760

Cone, J. D., & Foster, S. L. (1993). *Dissertation and theses from start to finish: Psychology and related fields.* American Psychological Association.

King, S. A., Kostewicz, D., Enders, O., Burch, T., Chitiyo, A., Taylor, J., DeMaria, S., & Reid, M. (2020). Search and selection procedures of literature reviews in behavior analysis. *Perspectives on Behavior Science, 43*(4), 725–760. doi:10.1007/s40614-020-00265-9

Luiselli, J. K. (2010). Writing for publication: A performance enhancement guide for the human services professional. *Behavior Modification, 34*(5), 459–473. doi:10.1177/0145445510383529

Normand, M. P., & Donohue, H. E. (2023). Research ethics for behavior analysts in practice. *Behavior Analysis in Practice*, *16*, 13–22. doi:10.1007/s40617-022-00698-5

Shawler, L. A., Blair, B. J., Harper, J. M., & Dorsey, M. F. (2018). A survey of the current state of the scientist-practitioner model in applied behavior analysis. *Education & Treatment of Children*, *41*(3), 277–297. doi:10.1353/etc.2018.0014

Sidman, M. (2011). Can an understanding of basic research facilitate the effectiveness of practitioners? Reflection and personal perspectives. *Journal of Applied Behavior Analysis*, *44*(4), 973–991. doi:10.1901/jaba.2011.44-973

Weiss, M. J. (2018). The concept of scientist practitioner and its extension to behavior analysis. *Education and Treatment of Children*, *41*(3), 385–394. doi:10.1353/etc.2018.0021

8 Writing as a Non-Human

Danielle Bratton

Artificial intelligence (AI), the driving force behind countless innovations, has found its way into the realm of writing. Behavior analysts can tap into AI to elevate their writing game in several key ways.

How AI Can Help

Automated Proofreading and Editing

AI-powered tools such as Grammarly and ProWritingAid are like vigilant guardians of your text, swiftly identifying and rectifying grammatical errors, improving sentence structures, and enhancing overall writing quality. This comes in especially handy when crafting assessment reports, progress notes, and research manuscripts. These tools can significantly enhance the quality of your writing by ensuring impeccable grammar, punctuation, and style. They catch errors that might be overlooked in manual proofreading, maintaining professionalism in your documents.

Natural Language Processing (NLP)

NLP technology is a game-changer for behavior analysts. It enables the analysis of vast troves of text, facilitating the extraction of invaluable insights. This tool is particularly useful for parsing through client records, spotting data trends, and generating relevant content for reports and research. NLP tools allow you to efficiently extract insights from large volumes of text, making data analysis more accessible. This can be a game-changer for research and assessment, saving time and providing a more comprehensive perspective.

Automated Report Generation

Say goodbye to tedious data extraction and report compilation. AI can take the reins, automatically organizing data and creating comprehensive assessment reports, progress reports, and treatment plans. This not only saves time but also guarantees accuracy and consistency. AI can streamline report generation, ensuring that your reports are consistent and accurate. This is particularly valuable in clinical settings, where time is of the essence.

Voice-to-Text Tools

In the age of AI, voice recognition software takes your spoken words and converts them into text swiftly and accurately. A behavior analyst can use this technology for transcribing session notes or conducting interviews with remarkable efficiency. Voice-to-text tools are a boon for efficiency, as they allow you to quickly convert spoken words into written text. This is especially useful for recording session notes and interviews, saving valuable time.

Best Practices for Using AI in Writing

To make the most of AI in your writing endeavors as a behavior analyst, it's imperative to adhere to some best practices.

Choose Your Tools Wisely

The first step is to select AI tools that align with your unique requirements. Depending on your needs, opt for AI-driven software designed to enhance written content or tailored for data analysis. By choosing the right tools, you can optimize your AI usage, ensuring that they cater to your specific needs, be it proofreading, data analysis, or report generation.

Writing as a Non-Human 117

Master the Tools

AI may be a technological marvel, but it requires some degree of mastery. Invest the time to understand how these tools work and how you can maximize their potential. Many AI platforms provide tutorials and resources to help you become proficient. Mastering AI tools allows you to leverage them effectively, increasing your productivity and the quality of your work.

Review AI-Generated Content

While AI can assist in generating content, it should never be a substitute for your expertise. Always review and refine AI-generated text to ensure its accuracy, relevance, and alignment with ethical considerations. AI-generated content can serve as a valuable starting point, saving time and effort in the writing process.

Uphold Ethical Standards

When using AI in behavior analysis, it is paramount to adhere to ethical standards governing client privacy and data security. Ensure that any data shared with AI tools are handled in compliance with the relevant regulations. Adhering to ethical standards safeguards client privacy and data security, ensuring that your use of AI is in line with professional guidelines.

Combine Human Expertise With AI

The most outstanding results often arise from the synergy between human expertise and AI. Use AI as a tool to enhance your work, not replace it. Remember that AI can't replicate the depth of understanding that a behavior analyst brings to the table. The combination of human expertise and AI's efficiency can result in high-quality work that leverages the best of both worlds.

Stay Updated

The field of AI is ever-evolving. Stay informed about the latest advancements and tools, ensuring that you remain at the forefront of AI utilization in behavior analysis. Keeping up with AI advancements ensures that you are making the most of the latest technology, improving your efficiency and the quality of your work.

Pitfalls and How Not to Use AI in Writing

While AI offers myriad advantages, it's essential to be aware of potential pitfalls and avoid misusing this technology.

Don't Over-Rely on AI

One of the most significant pitfalls is overreliance on AI tools. While they can undoubtedly improve your writing and data analysis, they should never supplant the judgment and expertise of a behavior analyst. Overreliance can lead to a loss of critical thinking and the human touch needed in behavior analysis.

Ethical Concerns Matter

Some AI tools may not fully grasp or respect the ethical considerations critical to behavior analysis, such as client confidentiality. It is crucial to stay vigilant and ensure that AI adheres to ethical standards.

Don't Skip the Review

Relying solely on AI-generated content without thorough review can result in inaccuracies and miscommunications. Always review and refine AI-generated work to maintain the highest standards of quality.

Understand How AI Works

Failing to understand how AI tools operate can lead to suboptimal use. Dedicate time to learning how these tools function, ensuring that you can harness their full potential. A lack of understanding can result in wasted time and resources.

Security and Privacy Concerns

Using AI tools that do not prioritize security and data privacy can lead to breaches and legal issues. Be cautious when choosing AI platforms and ensure they comply with relevant regulations.

Conclusion

The integration of artificial intelligence into behavior analysis offers exciting opportunities for enhancing written communication. AI can bolster efficiency, accuracy, and the overall quality of reports, research, and client communication. However, it is essential to approach AI as a valuable assistant rather than a replacement for human expertise. By following best practices, staying informed, and being aware of potential pitfalls, behavior analysts can leverage AI to their advantage while upholding ethical standards and delivering the best possible services to their clients. Recognizing the pitfalls and knowing how not to use AI are crucial for successfully navigating the world of AI-driven writing.

Do:

- Use AI to generate ideas or outlines for content.
- Word AI prompts to request short paragraphs to help you get started in your writing.
- Evaluate the results of generative AI content based on the literature to ensure accuracy.
- Consider if you need to cite the use of AI in your writing.

Don't:

- Copy AI-generated work directly without editing.
- Rely on AI to write your entire document.
- Assume that everything AI writes is accurate.
- Use AI to find references.

Self-Reflection Station

1 Reflect on this chapter. Did you recognize that it was entirely AI generated? Does this change your perspective on the information it provided?
2 In what ways can you use generative AI to support you in your work?

Practice: How Would You Respond?

1 Draft a presentation outline for a current project using generative AI. Review the outline and alter your AI prompt to improve the outline. Have the generative AI expand on the outline to include each component of the presentation and scholarly support. Conduct a thorough review of the information included and determine if the presentation meets professional and ethical standards as well as demonstrating compassion and general best practices.
2 Have generative AI draft a professional email for you. Alter the prompt to change the tone and incorporate soft skills in writing. Edit the email before sending. Based on how your recipient responds, evaluate the efficacy of your use of generative AI.

Note

This chapter was written by OpenAI (2023), based on the author's prompts, and then edited by the author.

Reference

OpenAI. (2023). ChatGPT (Nov 2 version) [Large language model]. https://chat.openai.com/chat

Appendix A: Words Matter

Correct Use of Terminology

ABA is filled with jargon. Sometimes, some of the terms are used incorrectly. Table A.1 includes common errors in ABA terminology, along with examples of how to use these terms correctly.

Table A.1 Correct ways to use ABA terminology.

Common Terminology Error	Correct Terminology Usage	Correct Example	Why Is This Correct?
Applied behavioral analysis	Applied behavior analysis	Applied behavior analysis is a science based on principles of operant conditioning.	The word "behavioral" modifies the word that follows it (i.e., analysis or analyst).
Behavioral analyst	Behavior analyst	The behavior analyst supervised her trainee every week.	The analyst performs an analysis of behavior, not an analysis done in a behavioral way.
Reinforcing a person	Reinforcing a behavior	Sitting independently was reinforced with screen time.	The process of reinforcement is defined by its effect on behavior, not people.
Prompting a person	Prompting a behavior	Manding was verbally prompted.	A prompt increases the likelihood of behavior, not people.

Common Terminology Error	Correct Terminology Usage	Correct Example	Why Is This Correct?
Data is	Data are	Data are collected on hand raising.	The word "data" is plural. If you are referring to a single piece of data, the word "datum" would be correct.
Behavior becomes extinct or is extinguished	Behavior is decreased through extinction	Calling out decreased after extinction was implemented.	Extinction is the process of no longer reinforcing behavior that had previously been reinforced. Even though behavior eventually decreases following extinction, there should not be an assumption that it will never occur again in the future.
Reinforcements	Reinforcers	Select reinforcers were provided when pictures were correctly labeled.	Reinforcement is the process of changing behavior. A reinforcer is the stimulus that is provided that increases the behavior.

Appendix B: Recommended Responses for "How Would You Respond?"

Chapter 1: Writing (and Communicating) as a Human

1. During our initial interview with the Langley family, you offered some good insights into the need for consistent scheduling as we set up their program. I want to give you some feedback about other supports that we can offer to parents during these early interactions after they receive a diagnosis for their child.

    In these situations, it is important to focus on offering compassionate care to address caregivers' concerns. When parents express their worries about their child's development, we should immediately acknowledge their feelings and validate their concerns. You can express empathy by saying, "I understand that this can be a challenging time for you, and it's natural to have concerns." We can then provide them with information about the diagnosis and the available resources, ensuring that we don't make unrealistic promises.

    Throughout the interview, we should encourage open communication, addressing any questions or concerns the parents have to build trust and establish a strong therapeutic alliance. It is crucial to emphasize the importance of setting realistic expectations, explaining that every child's progress is unique, and that improvement may take time and effort. To maintain an empathetic approach, we can incorporate techniques like motivational interviewing and compassion-oriented strategies.

    We also need to be mindful of language and terminology to reduce stigma and enhance rapport. By offering ongoing support with reasonable expectations, we can ensure that the parents understand the treatment process and feel adequately supported, which is essential for their child's progress. Compassionate care must remain a core principle throughout the interview, aiming to provide not only effective interventions but also emotional support to the families we work with.

2 Sarah, your expertise is unquestionable, and your insights are valuable. However, in our interactions, it's crucial to consider our audience. Using culturally responsive language and avoiding jargon can make our insights more accessible and enhance our professional image. Effective communication is clear and concise, without compromising precision. Credibility is vital, and we can maintain it by consistently showcasing our expertise through well-researched content and transparent communication.

Furthermore, respectful communication is at the heart of building strong relationships within our community. We should acknowledge and value diverse perspectives and avoid dismissive language, prioritizing active listening and empathy. These principles not only shape our perception but also contribute to a culture of collaboration and shared growth.

Chapter 2: Writing as a Student

1 Thank you for sharing your perspective on this topic. It's evident that this issue generates diverse opinions. I respectfully disagree and would like to offer a behavior analytic viewpoint supported by published research. In a study conducted by [insert citation], they found that [brief summary of the findings]. This aligns with the behavior analytic principles of [mention the relevant principles]. I believe this approach is more effective because [explain your rationale based on the research].

I appreciate your willingness to engage in this discussion, and I look forward to further dialogue. Are there specific concerns or questions about the behavior analytic approach that you'd like to explore further?

2 Dear Professor,

I hope this email finds you well. I wanted to discuss my recent assignment grade and the feedback provided. First, I want to express my appreciation for your guidance and the opportunity to learn and grow in this course. After reviewing your feedback and carefully reassessing my assignment, I believe that I have addressed all the assignment components as outlined in the instructions. Based on my recalculation, it appears that I should earn 20 additional points, which would bring my grade from 70% to 90%.

I understand that grades are earned, and I want to ensure that I have met the course competencies and criteria. If I have overlooked any specific requirements, I would appreciate your guidance on what I could have done differently. I truly value your expertise and feedback, and I want to ensure that I am meeting the standards set for this course.

I kindly request your reconsideration of my assignment, and if possible, a review of the components that I believe have been met. I understand the importance of course assessments and want to ensure that I am aligned with your expectations.

Thank you for your time and consideration, and I look forward to your response. If you need any additional information or clarification from me, please don't hesitate to ask.
Sincerely
[Your name]

Chapter 3: Writing as a Clinician

1 Clarify service descriptions: Ensure that service descriptions accurately reflect the nature of the services provided. Be precise in describing the activities, interventions, and interactions that took place during the session. If there are discrepancies between what was done and what is documented, it can lead to billing inaccuracies and a lack of transparency.

 Avoid duplicated content: Each session is unique, and the documentation should reflect the specific details and progress made during that session. Duplicated content can lead to misunderstandings and hinder the ability to track a client's progress accurately.

Individualized notes: Session notes must be tailored to each client's needs and progress. Using examples as guides is acceptable but should not lead to a copy-and-paste approach.

Timely documentation: Complete session notes in real time whenever possible. This approach ensures that the documentation accurately captures the events and interventions as they occur. Delayed documentation may lead to inaccuracies and gaps in the client's record.

2 Can you describe a recent situation when your child started hitting or attempting to hit? What was happening, and how did it unfold?

How do you and your child typically handle situations that seem to trigger the hitting behavior? Can you walk me through, step by step, how you responded to hitting?

In your opinion, what do you think your child might be trying to communicate or achieve when they resort to hitting? Are there specific patterns or triggers you've noticed that precede these episodes?

Chapter 4: Writing as a Leader

1 I want to express my appreciation for your suggestion to include the brushing and joint compression intervention in the client's daily routine to address disruptive behavior. However, I have some concerns that I'd like to discuss in a professional and constructive manner, keeping in mind the need for effective interdisciplinary communication.

While I acknowledge the potential benefits of the intervention as we have seen, it's important for me to be mindful of the ethical code of conduct I must follow and adhere to evidence-based practices that are within my scope of competence. As a behavior analyst, these interventions are outside my scope of practice, and I am unable to participate.

In approaching this situation, I would like to propose that we work together to identify strategies that are effective, within our respective scopes of practice, and are ethically sound.

I value your input as a valued member of our interdisciplinary team and look forward to collaborating to find the most appropriate and effective solution for our client's needs.

2 I have recently become aware of concerns regarding my collaboration with the team, and I want to address these concerns in a manner that promotes better working relationships and more effective interdisciplinary collaboration. I understand that there have been concerns raised about my communication style; specifically, that I may come across as dismissive of your concerns and ideas. I want to sincerely apologize that my previous interactions have communicated this, as it was never my intention.

I greatly value the contributions of each team member and firmly believe that the best outcomes are achieved when we work together, drawing on our collective expertise. In light of this feedback, I am eager to improve our collaboration and create a more inclusive and supportive environment for everyone. I would be grateful for any specific feedback or suggestions you may have on how I can enhance my approach and better contribute to the team's objectives. Your input is invaluable in helping me become a more effective and considerate team member.

Thank you for your understanding, and I look forward to your insights as we continue working together.

Chapter 5: Writing as a Supervisor

1 Express understanding and empathy: I would begin by acknowledging the supervisee's feelings and concerns. I might say something like, "I appreciate your honesty in sharing your thoughts and feelings about our supervision meetings. I understand that you may have some reservations about my feedback, and I want to address them."

Clarify expectations: I would then clarify the expectations for supervision. I'd explain the importance of regular and punctual attendance, as well as active participation, in order to maximize the benefits of the supervision process. This would include emphasizing the need for open communication.

Seek specific feedback: I would ask the supervisee for specific examples or instances where they felt my feedback was and was not helpful. This could help pinpoint areas for improvement in my supervisory approach. For example, I might ask, "Can you provide me with some specific examples or situations where you found my feedback less effective or unhelpful, so that I can start to adjust my approach for the best possible outcome for you?"

Listen actively: I would actively listen to the supervisee's response without interruption, ensuring that they have the opportunity to express their concerns fully. This demonstrates that I value their perspective.

Collaborative problem-solving: Once I have a clear understanding of the supervisee's concerns, I would propose a collaborative problem-solving approach. We could discuss potential changes or adjustments to our supervision process that might address their needs and concerns while still meeting the requirements of the training program.

Feedback on feedback: I would also inquire about the supervisee's preferred feedback style and what kind of feedback they find most helpful. This information can guide me in providing more effective feedback tailored to their learning style.

Set clear expectations: I would reiterate the importance of professionalism, punctuality, and active participation during our supervision meetings. Setting clear expectations for future meetings can help prevent similar issues from arising.

Follow-up plan: Finally, I would suggest a follow-up meeting to assess whether the adjustments made have improved the supervisee's experience with supervision and if they find the feedback more helpful.

This approach aims to create a collaborative and supportive supervisory relationship that addresses the concerns raised by the graduate student while maintaining a focus on their professional development and adherence to behavior analysis principles.

2. Dear Luisa,

I hope this message finds you well. I want to begin by expressing my appreciation for the outstanding work you've been doing as a paraprofessional within our school's special education program. Your dedication and commitment to implementing behavior intervention strategies for students with special needs have not gone unnoticed, and I am delighted to provide you with feedback and documentation of your performance.

Your success as a paraprofessional has been evident through the following accomplishments:

- Exceptional intervention skills: Your ability to implement behavior intervention strategies effectively has made a significant positive impact on the students under your care. You've consistently demonstrated a deep understanding of behavior analytic principles and their practical application.
- Collaborative spirit: Your willingness to collaborate with other team members, including teachers, therapists, and fellow paraprofessionals, has greatly enhanced the overall quality of support and services provided to our students. Your teamwork and open communication have been invaluable.
- Dedication and professionalism: Your dedication to your role as a paraprofessional has been exemplary. You consistently go above and beyond to ensure that students' needs are met, and your professionalism in the school environment sets a high standard for others to follow.

While your performance has been outstanding, there are a few areas where continued growth and training may be beneficial:

- Expanding knowledge: Consider broadening your knowledge in behavior analysis by pursuing additional training or coursework. This could include exploring advanced topics in behavior analysis, which will further enhance your effectiveness in supporting students.
- Data collection and analysis: Enhance your skills in data collection and analysis to provide even more precise feedback on student progress. This will help in refining your intervention strategies and measuring their effectiveness.
- Self-reflection: Continue to engage in self-reflection and self-assessment regarding your practices. This self-awareness will allow you to identify areas where you can make further improvements and adjustments.

I want to emphasize that the feedback provided here is in line with the best practices and ethical standards associated with supervision in behavior analysis. All written documentation, including this evaluation report, is intended to be technological, informative, and culturally responsive, just as outlined in the guidelines you're familiar with.

Please feel free to share your thoughts, questions, or suggestions on this feedback. Your input is essential to creating a collaborative and effective supervisory relationship. We can also discuss your thoughts during our next scheduled supervisory meeting.

Luisa, I'm excited about your potential for continuous development and the positive impact you will continue to have on the students in our school. Your growth as a paraprofessional is not only a credit to your hard work but also to the valuable support you provide to our students with special needs.

Thank you for your dedication to the well-being and development of our students. I look forward to seeing your continued growth and success.

Chapters 6, 7, and 8

Owing to the nature of the "How Would You Respond" questions in these chapters, no example answers are provided. Please use the questions from these chapters to reflect on situations from your own experiences.

Index

advocacy work 61–65
AI 116–120
analyzing research 21–22
assessment: descriptive 33–34; indirect 32–33; reports 31, 38–40; skills 36–38
assignments 16–19, 25–27, 86–87
autoclitics 7
automated report generation 116

Behavior Analysis Certification Board Code of Ethics xv
blog posts 1

caregivers: communicating with 51–57; session notes 47–49
citing sources 2, 23
clinical documentation 45
clinician (writing as a): documentation of services 41–42, 44–49; functional analysis 34–36; goals 40–41; interpretations 38–40; overview 30–31; progress reports 42–44; recommendations 39–40; session notes 44–49; *see also* assessment
communication, importance of xiii–xiv
compare and contrast 21
compassionate practice xv, 6–8
compassion-focused communication 51–54
conference presentations 105–109
confidentiality 3
context, importance of 2
contract, in supervision 73
corrective feedback 25–27, 77–78
course content writing 84–86
credibility 4
critical thinking 20–22

databases 93
defining/describing 20
descriptive assessments 33–34
digital databases 93
discussion boards 13–16
documentation of services 41–42

editing 115
email communication 11–13
empathy 6–8, 51–52
ethics: AI 117, 118; in social media communication 2–3
evaluation of supervision 75–80
evidence-based support 66–67

faculty member (writing as a): assignment instructions 86–87; course content 84–86; providing feedback 25–27, 87–89; syllabus 83–84

feedback: corrective (students) 25–27, 87–89; performance 54–56; in supervision 75–80
follow-up documentation 56–57
functional analysis 34–36
funders 65–67

goals 40–41
grammar 22–24
grant proposals 101–105

honesty 22–24

identity versus disability-first language 7
indirect assessments 32–33
interdisciplinary teams communication 58–60
interpretations in assessment reports 38–40

jargon 4, 52, 53, 121–122
journal articles 110–112

literature reviews 91–92, 93–98
lobbying work 61–65

medical providers 65–67
misconceptions, addressing 62, 63
moderation (online) 2

natural language processing (NLP) 115–116
non-behavioral colleagues 58–60

observations of behavior 33–34
outcome projections 66

paraphrasing 22–23
"parent training" 47–49
patient-centered approaches 67
performance feedback 54–56, 76–78
person-first language 7
plagiarism 22
policy makers, communicating with 60–65

poster presentations 106–107
privacy, on social media 3
professionalism in online discussions 2
professional organization membership 5
progress reports 42–44
pronouns 7
proofreading 24–25, 115
proposals: grant 101–105; research 98–101
public perception 4–6
public relations problem xiv–xv, 61

quantitative vs. qualitative data 63

recommendations 39–40, 54–56
references: on social media 2; in student writing 23
researcher (writing as a): conference presentations 105–109; evaluating studies 96; grant proposals 101–105; identifying articles for review 94–95; identifying the research topic 92; identifying search criteria 93–94; journal articles 110–112; literature reviews 91–92, 93–98; organizing the articles 95–96; poster presentations 106–107; research proposals 98–101; slide presentations 107–108; symposia 109; synthesizing information 96–98; webinars 109–110; workshops 108–109
respectful communication 5, 59–60

Session Notes 44–49
skills assessment 36–38
slide presentations 107–108
social media 1–3
special interest groups (SIG) 5
student writing: assignments 16–19; critical thinking 20–22; discussion boards 13–16; email communication 11–13; grammar

22–24; honesty in 22–24; proofreading 24–25; responding to corrective feedback 25–27; writing style 22–24
summarizing research 20–21
supervisor (writing as a): contracts 73; evaluations/feedback 75–80; meeting documentation 74–75; overview 70–71; structured behavior analytic content 71–72
syllabus writing 83–84
symposia 109

synthesizing research 21

team language 52–53
team members (non-behavioral) 58–60
terminology 121–122
therapeutic alliance 7

visibility 5
voice-to-text tools 116

webinars 109–110
workshops 108–109